Damn Near White

Damn Near White

An African American Family's Rise
from Slavery to Bittersweet Success

Carolyn Marie Wilkins

University of Missouri Press   Columbia and London

Copyright © 2010 by
Carolyn Marie Wilkins
University of Missouri Press, Columbia, Missouri 65201
Printed and bound in the United States of America
All rights reserved
5 4 3 2 1   14 13 12 11 10

Cataloging-in-Publication data available from the Library of Congress

ISBN 978-0-8262-1899-5

®™ This paper meets the requirements of the
American National Standard for Permanence of Paper
for Printed Library Materials, Z39.48, 1984.

Jacket design: Kristie Lee
Interior design and composition: Jennifer Cropp
Printing and binding: Thomson-Shore, Inc.
Typefaces: Minion and Bodoni

This book is dedicated to my family—
past, present and future.

We Wear the Mask

We wear the mask that grins and lies,
It hides our cheeks and shades our eyes,
This debt we pay to human guile;
With torn and bleeding hearts we smile,
And mouth with myriad subtleties.
Why should the world be over-wise,
In counting all our tears and sighs?
Nay, let them only see us, while
We wear the mask.

Paul Laurence Dunbar (1872–1906)
"We Wear the Mask"

Contents

Acknowledgments

The Africans say that it takes a village to raise a child. In creating this book, I am fortunate to have had the assistance of my own village of supporters. Mariah Cooper persisted doggedly until she was able to uncover long-buried family secrets; Lolita Paiewonsky and Christen Enos read my early drafts and helped me find my writing voice; Mr. Clair Willcox, Sara Davis and the rest of the people at the University of Missouri Press provided invaluable editorial support.

I owe an enormous debt of gratitude to Mrs. Laranita Dougas, Reverend Theodore Hesburgh, Judge George N. Leighton, James Montgomery, Esq., Mr. Rocco Siciliano, and Judge Anna Diggs Taylor for taking time out of their busy schedules to share their memories of J. Ernest Wilkins with me.

I would also like to thank the many librarians and archivists who helped me in my quest: Carmen Beck, Lincoln University; Robin Beck, University of Illinois; Diane Black, Tennessee State Library Archives; Frances Bristol, Archives of The United Methodist Church; Robin Charlaw, Harvard University Archives; Jean Church, Howard University; Katherine Collett, Hamilton College Library; Julia Gardner, University of Chicago Library; Fred Gillespie, Pilgrim Baptist Church; Daniel Hartwig, Yale University Archives; Michelle Kopfer, Dwight D. Eisenhower Archives; William J. Maher, University of Illinois at Urbana-Champaign; Katie Mc Mahon, Newberry Library; Amber Miranda, Southeastern Missouri State University; Karen Roman, Travis Trokey, Farmington Public Library; Andrea Savoy, Cynthia Weidner, Sigma Pi Phi Archives; Jessie Carney Smith, Fisk University and Linda Stinson at the Department of Labor Archives.

I am grateful for the help of my Farmington friends Bill Matthews, Vonne Phillips, Bob Lewis and Faye Sitzes, and my Oxford friends Hollis Crowder and Joan Bratton at the Skipwith Historical Society, for sharing their files, research acumen and stories with me.

I'd also like to extend a warm thank-you to Dr. James "Chris" Wright and his family. I am especially grateful for having had the chance to correspond with Mrs. Ethel Porter before she died.

My family has been incredible. Aunt Connie and Mom patiently answered my many questions for hours on end. David, Ann Marie, Timothy, Stephen,

Emelda, Sally, Jason, Rebecca and Lance each offered love, ideas, encouragement and support. My daughter Sarah's insightful comments gave me much-needed perspective, while my husband, John, stood by me every step of the way. Without his research expertise, creative input and sustaining love, the book you now hold in your hands would still be a sheaf of pages buried at the bottom of my desk drawer.

Author's Note

Some of the quotations in this book contain misspellings and other grammatical errors. In order to give the reader a feel for the characters in my story and the times in which they lived, I have chosen to reproduce these quotes, mistakes and all, exactly as they originally appeared.

Damn Near White

Wilkins family, 1965 (left to right): Mom, Timothy, Stephen, Carolyn, David, Dad

Chapter One

The Black Bourgeois Blues

That girl was staring at me, I could feel it from across the room. Tugging surreptitiously at the hem of my miniskirt, I pushed my way through the crowd and poured myself another drink from the makeshift bar. A second paper cupful of cheap Chianti did little to relieve my anxiety.

I didn't know a soul in the room.

It was September 1969, and I was attending my first-ever party as a college student. I had never lived away from home before, and hard as I was trying to hide it, I had never tasted an alcoholic drink before that night. More than anything, I wanted to be as cool as the other longhaired, blue-jeaned flower children who filled the small apartment.

Jefferson Airplane's music poured from a colossal speaker propped on a milk crate in the corner. "Don't you want somebody to love? Don't you need somebody to love?" screamed Grace Slick. Yes I did. Desperately.

Clutching my drink, I took a deep breath and headed toward the kitchen. When I turned around, the girl was standing right in front of me. She was staring even harder.

"What are you?" she said, inspecting me through her granny glasses.

"Excuse me?"

"What are you? You know, what country are you from?"

"I'm American. I was born in Chicago."

"Oh." Clearly unsatisfied, she twirled a lock of strawberry blonde hair between her fingers. "You know what I mean. I mean, what ethnicity are you?"

Here we go again, I thought. A familiar knot began to tighten in my gut. I looked around for someone else to talk to, but the girl had planted herself directly in my path. There was no escape.

"I'm black," I replied, using the terminology of the day.

A wrinkle of irritation creased her face and twisted her thin lips into a pout.

1

"No you're not," she said. "Your skin is nowhere near black. You're more like tan. Are you Israeli?"

"I told you, I'm black." My mother had raised me to be polite to strangers, but this was getting ridiculous. The girl's high twangy voice reverberated across the room, and a small crowd began to gather.

"I know. One of your parents must be white, then," an onlooker piped up.

"You definitely don't talk like a black person," offered another voice from the back of the room.

"Yeah. You don't even have a southern accent."

This was getting way out of hand.

"No. I'm black. Both my parents are black. My whole family is black. Excuse me." Abandoning all hope of ever fitting in with this crowd, I pushed past my tormentors and fled into the crisp September night.

In the forty years that have passed since this incident, I have had to explain my racial background to curious strangers on a fairly regular basis. When I was growing up, my parents bypassed the Chicago public school system and placed me in an elite private academy where I studied side by side with the children of University of Chicago professors. My family lived in an integrated neighborhood, and my brothers and I played with white, black, and Asian kids as equals.

Although I now have good friends of all colors, there is no denying that much of my life has been spent straddling the racial divide. Some of the most painful rejections of my blackness have come not from whites, whose ignorance on the subject of racial identity is at least somewhat understandable, but from my fellow blacks. My first serious boyfriend was a dark-skinned black militant from the slums of North Philadelphia. He loved my yellow skin and long hair, in private, but when his friends saw us out walking in the 'hood one day, they thought I was a white girl and taunted him about it later. My boyfriend was horrified. Desperate to please him, I cut my shoulder-length hair into an Afro the very next day, but the damage had been done. He dumped me within a matter of weeks.

As I grew to adulthood, these and other incidents left me scarred and confused. Who was I, really? Where did I truly belong? When I chose to marry a white man, the cloud of racial angst swirling around me thickened. The idea that I could be both proud of my African American roots and in love with someone of another race upset folks on both sides of the color line.

Even when they don't know about my interracial marriage, some people refuse to believe I am black. My wavy hair, light complexion, and private school vocabulary confuses them, threatening their stereotypical concepts of African Americans. Since I look and act so "white," why on earth would I insist on calling myself black?

This identity crisis would not have been an issue for my parents. They knew who they were. When Mom and Dad grew up in the 1940s, there was little social contact between whites and blacks. De facto segregation was in full force, even in the big northern cities, and the kind of interracial college party I attended in 1969 would have been extremely rare.

My mother tells a story about the first time she met her roommate at Smith College. The girl was white, from a wealthy New England family. As Mom got ready to go to bed that night, she noticed that her roommate was staring at her. Feeling more than a little self-conscious, my mother finally asked the girl what she was looking at. The roommate sheepishly replied that she was looking for Mom's tail. She had heard that all black people had tails and, never having been this close to a black person before, she wanted to see if the story was true.

During the 1950s blacks were routinely discriminated against in virtually every area of American life. When my parents were in college, African American students were often excluded from collegiate social events. White fraternities and sororities in the North as well as in the South barred black students from membership. My parents' generation responded by creating their own alternative world of all-black social organizations. There were hundreds of African American social clubs and women's groups; there were black fraternities and sororities. And black folks have run their own churches since before the end of slavery.

Within this all-black world, there were many layers and levels of prestige. The criteria for who would get admitted and who would get excluded from the top tier of black society were based on a complex mixture of wealth, social influence, and family connections. Skin color was very important. For the social climber trying to enter black society, a light complexion, while not an absolute requirement, gave one a huge advantage. Back in the day, black folks had a saying: "If you're white, you're alright. If you're brown, stick around. If you're black, get back."

In *Black Bourgeoisie*, his scathing 1957 study of African American middle-class social mores, the black sociologist E. Franklin Frazier described the "unavowed color snobbishness" and insular tendencies he found within many black organizations. Blacks participated in "society" activities not simply for social reasons, Frazier observed, but "in order to maintain status or as a part of the competition for status." In Frazier's view, the driving rationale behind the creation of an alternative elite world of black bourgeois social activities was to differentiate these bourgeois blacks "from the masses of poorer Negroes and at the same time compensate for the exclusion of the black bourgeoisie from the larger white community."[1]

When it came to differentiating themselves from the majority of Chicago's African Americans in 1950, the Wilkins family stood near the top of the social ladder. My paternal grandfather, J. Ernest Wilkins, was a successful attorney, a powerful figure in the Kappa Alpha Psi fraternity, and an active member in Sigma Pi Phi, an invitation-only society for African American men of distinction. He and his pale-skinned blue-eyed wife, Lucile, were among the rarified handful of blacks with advanced degrees from the University of Chicago.

Each of J. Ernest and Lucile's three sons was distinguished in his own right. My father, Julian, was a Harvard Law graduate and a successful attorney. His brother John, also a Harvard Law graduate, worked for the Justice Department in Washington. And my uncle J. Ernest Wilkins Jr. was a physics prodigy and earned a Ph.D. from the University of Chicago at the age of nineteen. No one on the Wilkins side of the family featured a skin color darker than almond.

My mother's family, the Sweeneys, had amassed their own string of accomplishments. My grandfather Rev. Samuel Sweeney, pastor of the largest Methodist church in Harlem, was an Oberlin graduate who spoke Greek and Latin. Before my mother was allowed to marry my father, her parents made her promise that she would finish her education. For the first six months of her married life, Mom dutifully finished up her master's degree in musicology at Smith College in Massachusetts while my father waited back home in Chicago.

The Wilkins family's star rose even higher in the black bourgeois firmament when my grandfather J. Ernest Wilkins was appointed U.S. assistant secretary of labor in 1954. My grandfather was the first black man ever to participate in a Cabinet meeting and was sent abroad to represent the United States at labor conferences in Europe and the Caribbean. His groundbreaking appointment made front-page news in newspapers across the country. In 1957 J. Ernest again made history when he served as the lone black member on the first U.S. Civil Rights Commission.

As I was coming of age in the 1960s, however, times were changing. With the coming of integration, the tight-knit world of the black elite, while it didn't entirely fade away, lost its place as the sole arbiter of social success. A new militancy was sweeping through the black community, and in many quarters a light complexion was no longer such a desirable commodity. By the time I entered college, "Black" had become "Beautiful." Afros were in, and "high yellow" blacks like me scrambled to prove that, despite our light skin, we were "down with the Revolution."

Despite the winds of change blowing through their color-conscious world, however, my parents held fast to the old values. When I was a kid they dragged me kicking and screaming to meetings of the elite Jack and Jill Club, in the hopes that I would begin to make the proper social contacts early in life. When I turned sixteen, my folks deposited a hefty sum of money with the Links Society so that I could "come out" in the prestigious organization's annual spring debutante ball.

For months leading up to the cotillion, my fellow debutantes and I lived in a bizarre time warp. In a large ballroom deep on Chicago's South Side, we put our modern selves aside. Dressed in our Sunday best, we perched daintily on the edges of our chairs while doddering blue-haired ladies with skin the color of almond paste lectured us on the arcane niceties of proper etiquette. I learned what all the forks were for, how to address a duke or an earl in case I happened to meet one, and most important, how to curtsey. Every Saturday for months under the watchful eyes of these women, my long-suffering boyfriend and I practiced our minuets, waltzes, and the most sedate cha-cha you ever saw west of Buckingham Palace.

No one darker than a paper bag joined our little soirees. Our clothing, hair-styles, and demeanor were inspected weekly to ensure compliance with "proper" bourgeois social standards. One girl showed up for practice in an Afro one day. She was quietly taken aside and asked to leave the group. When the night of the Big Dance finally arrived, my parents beamed with pride from the front row as my fellow debutantes and I, attired in formal gowns and sixteen-button gloves, waltzed awkwardly around the room on the arms of our escorts. All told, my experience as a black debutante ranks among the most miserable moments of my life. If this was what my family's black heritage was all about, I wanted no part of it.

However, there was someone in my family who had not allowed the social conventions demanded by "proper" black society to limit her. Despite her status as the "grand dame" of our extended family clan, my father's Aunt Marjory had managed to retain her earthy vitality. When I was around her, I felt connected to a family history that was about much more than prestige and material success. Because her sister had been married to my famous grandfather J. Ernest Wilkins, Aunt Marjory was technically my great-aunt. But most people who knew her, even those who were not relatives, just called her Aunt Marj.

By the time I got to know her, Aunt Marj was already in her late eighties. She felt she had earned the right to say and do just about whatever she wanted. Her sharp tongue and eccentric ways were legendary, as were her warmth and generosity.

One thing that Aunt Marjory and I had in common was music. She played the piano, composed, and sang, just as I did. Back in the 1920s she had studied at the prestigious Conservatorio di Guiseppe Verdi in Milan, where Giacomo Puccini, Gian Carlo Menotti, and a host of Italy's most respected composers and conductors had received their training. A true citizen of the world, Aunt Marj spoke Italian and at least three other languages. When she came back to the States she founded the J. Marjory Jackson Academy of the Arts, which thrived in the heart of Brooklyn's tough Bedford Stuyvesant neighborhood for the next fifty years. Although her eyesight was failing, Aunt Marjory remained active, still teaching music, Spanish, and French to a motley crew of preschoolers in her basement.

A four-foot-ten-inch bundle of dynamite, Aunt Marj had never met a crowd she couldn't entertain. One Christmas Eve when she was on her way from New York to Chicago, a snowstorm grounded her plane for several hours. Family legend has it that Aunt Marj, unfazed, unpacked a small portable keyboard and proceeded to entertain the stranded passengers until the plane was able to take off again.

Never content merely to drift through life, she was always up for an adventure. Even at eighty-five, when her diet consisted largely of instant mashed potatoes and orange soda, she talked of taking a trip to Europe "sometime soon," to sit along the great boulevards of Paris and watch the people. "And you know what I'm going to do?" she'd say with a glint in her eye. "I'm going to get a gigolo to keep me company. Just you wait and see!"

Aunt Marjory had always been one to extend a helping hand to anyone who needed it, especially family members. She was the Queen, the Matriarch, and if you were hurting, for whatever reason, she was the one you went to for an encouraging word. Each Thanksgiving, she'd invite twenty friends and family members to share the holiday with her. And, after every Thanksgiving dinner, she'd remind all the family members that our ancestors came from Africa.

With her chest puffed out and her head up high, Aunt Marjory would declaim in her most resonant tones. "More than two hundred years ago your ancestor Jeremiah came to New York on a slave ship from Madagascar. He docked at Fulton Street right here in Brooklyn." At this point in her narrative, she would cock her head and look at each of us in turn.

"I'll bet you didn't even know that they had a slave market here. But they did. Jeremiah was sold at a slave auction to a man named Robinson and went to live in Kentucky. He was a slave. But he escaped! He followed the Underground Railroad to freedom in Calgary, Canada. There he met a beautiful Indian woman from the Saskatoon tribe and they married. This is the beginning of our family. We came from Africa, but now we live all over the world."

At every family gathering, Aunt Marj would tell the story of Jeremiah and our African ancestors. She would speak of the trials they endured during slavery, and of our vast extended family, which now included just about every race and color under the sun. Then she would have us sing Sister Sledge's "We Are Family." Which was pretty funny, because these were the only words any of us ever learned to that song. We'd just repeat it over and over again in a joyous raucous chorus. Stomping our feet and clapping along, we'd all belt it out together: "We are family! We are family! We are family!"

Aunt Marj tried her best to pass along her encyclopedic knowledge of family lore to the next generation. I cannot remember any visit to her brownstone that did not include a lengthy session with her photo albums.

"Listen, Carolyn," she would say. "Go in my study and bring me my albums."

Dutifully, I would rise from the overstuffed sofa and squeeze into the cramped room that she used as a study. The room was six feet wide at best. On the desk at the end of the room sat a small typewriter and a Dictaphone, buried under tottering piles of paper. The shelves lining the walls on both sides of the room sagged under the weight of Aunt Marj's memorabilia. There was her doll collection, scores of dolls in their native costumes from all over the world. There were the statues, and delicate figurines, and glass paperweights, given as gifts by grateful students. There were plaques, and framed photos of Aunt Marj with mayors, congressmen, students, and friends.

And then there were the photo albums. Ten bulging volumes. A lifetime of memories.

Carefully I pried one loose from between a glass ballerina and a stack of old vinyl record albums.

"Here we are," I said, carrying it back to the living room and placing it between us on the sofa.

"This is your family, Carolyn. We come from every continent on this planet. It's very important to know who you are and who your family is."

For the next three hours, we'd go through the scrapbooks one by one. You could see the years drop away as she lovingly turned the pages. None of the pictures was labeled, but Aunt Marj knew who and what was in each snapshot.

Here was Uncle Charles, her ne'er-do-well brother who, according to Aunt Marj, had himself buried faced down so that the entire world could "kiss his you-know-what."

Here was Aunt Francis, the Liberian orphan that Aunt Marj's father adopted during a missionary trip to Africa in the 1930s.

Here was Aunt Marj walking down the streets of Milan with her schoolmates at the Conservatorio in 1921.

The list went on and on. Each picture was important, and each one told a story. At the end of a few hours with her photo albums, my head would be spinning. "Some day, I really should write down those stories," I'd say to myself. "Oh well. I will definitely do it the next time I visit."

I guess all of us thought Aunt Marj was indestructible. After all, she was nearly ninety years old and just as spunky as ever. But one sweltering day in June 1995, she slipped and fell and broke her hip in two places. When she recovered, the family heaved a collective sigh of relief. But a few weeks later, Aunt Marj was back in the hospital. This time she had pneumonia.

By the next week she was gone, her body reduced to a pile of cellophane-wrapped ashes in a cardboard box. In a matter of weeks Aunt Marjory's Brooklyn brownstone was cleaned out and sold. My brother Stephen took the elegant dining-room table where we had shared so many Thanksgiving memories. My brother David took her 1908 Steinway grand. I wanted it, but it was too massive to fit in my living room. My brother Timothy took what was left of her vintage silver.

And I took the scrapbooks.

Ironically, this keeper of the family legacy had made no provision for her own final resting place. Until a proper burial spot could be arranged, I agreed to keep the box holding her ashes. J. Marjory Jackson's journey was over. But my journey of discovery had just begun.

John and Abu in Prospect Park

Chapter Two

The Research Begins, 1995

I grieved Aunt Marjory's death for months. She had been my living history book; she made me feel I was attached to something larger than my immediate family. Other family members were hurting, too. My brothers and I talked fondly of the big Thanksgiving dinners she used to give. From time to time at family gatherings, we would all burst out singing "We Are Family" in Aunt Marj's memory.

As the weeks following her passing stretched into months, everyone returned to their own busy lives. My brother David, a professor at Harvard Law School, was soliciting funding for a new center he'd created for the study of global legal issues. My brother Timothy was a partner at a high-powered law firm in New York City. My brother Stephen ran the elementary school sports department for the Chicago public school system.

As a music teacher and semi-employed jazz musician, I was the one with the most time to brood. When Thanksgiving came and went without the usual visit to Aunt Marjory's Brooklyn brownstone, I sat down and made a list of all the questions I should have asked her while she was alive:

Who were my father's people and how did I come by the name Wilkins?
Were they slaves on a plantation? If so, where? What did they do?
What part of Africa had they come from?
Were there white people in my family tree, and if so, how did they get there?
Were there Native Americans? If so, what tribe?

The list went on in this vein for several pages. When I was finished writing, I put my head down and cried. With Aunt Marjory's passing, the last and maybe the only person who knew the intimate details of our family's history was gone.

I spent hours at the piano, trying to work through my grief. I would play Aunt Marj's favorite spirituals over and over again while I pondered. Humming along as I played "Balm in Gilead" or "Swing Low, Sweet Chariot," I would wonder, what was the world like when she first heard these songs? Who sang them to her as a child? Aunt Marjory had loved to talk about her father, Rev. John Wallace Robinson, who had pastored St. Mark's Church in Harlem during the 1920s. She had been so connected, so rooted in her world, her heritage, and her religion.

Sadly, I contemplated my own spotty relationship to the Christian church. The last time I could remember even going to church other than to play a gig had been for an Easter service more than five years before. Lately I had found myself yearning for a deeper connection, both to my Christian heritage and to my African roots.

More months passed. I joined a group of Cubans who practiced Santeria, an amalgam of Catholicism and African animism. We dressed in white, danced to pounding conga drums, and practiced animal sacrifice. We spent hours in the woods connecting with nature spirits, bathed naked in the river at midnight, and collected dirt from graves in the local cemetery. My family and friends were appalled at my new activities. My husband, John, seriously considered a divorce.

It was a time of intense spiritual and personal questioning for me. Surely there was a larger purpose for my presence on this earth than simply to pursue my own selfish desires? Who was I really? What was my purpose in being here?

Despite the adamant objections of my family and friends, I felt strongly drawn to African spirituality. In Santeria, as in many traditional African religions, God is not in intimate contact with His creation. Santeria's practitioners believe that there are seven major energy forces, called Orisas, that govern the material world as God's intermediaries. Every Santeria initiate is believed to have a special relationship with one of the Orisas. This Orisa is that person's Guardian Angel, guiding them and protecting them through life. When I announced my intention to learn more about my Guardian Angel, a wizened Cuban divination specialist was brought up from New York to do a "reading" for me.

After a brand new one-hundred-dollar bill ritually wrapped in aluminum foil had changed hands, a white dove was sacrificed, and I was washed in a special bath made from secret herbs. Then, dressed in a brand new white gown, I was led into my sponsor's kitchen. As I squatted on the spotless linoleum floor, the tiny old man shifted a pair of worn kola nuts from one hand to another to read the signs. Looking on, I was transported across oceans and centuries.

When it was all over, I learned that Olokùn, the energy of the depths of the sea, was my guiding Orisa. Since Santeria practitioners believe that the energy of Olokùn is too strong to be taken in directly, I would be initiated into the mysteries of Yemayà, the goddess of oceans and motherhood. Before receiving the spiritual energy of Yemaya, my Santeria elders advised me to establish a connection with my ancestors.

On the night before my initiation, the members of my Santeria group held a séance to let my ancestors know about the big step I was about to take. The ceremony took place late at night in the home of the Santeria priest who would initiate me the next day. After having received a ritual bath made from herbs and flowers, I was doused in Florida Water, a pungent cologne believed to have spiritual power. I was dressed in a long white robe and placed in the center of a circle. As I fell into a light trance, the other members of my group gathered around me, dancing and singing to the ancestors. The small inner city apartment was alive with energy and thick with the smell of Florida Water, incense, and sweat.

It was about three o'clock in the morning, and we had been going at it for several hours. Suddenly the music and movement around me stopped. My mouth opened, and I began to sing.

The voice coming out of me was completely outside my control, utterly unlike any singing I had ever done before. Someone else was singing through me, and it was beautiful! I don't know how long I sang, or what song it was, but after that moment I was never the same.

That Singer was the voice of my ancestors, and I knew then that I was deeply and inextricably connected to them. I believed that somewhere out in the ether, my ancestors were watching and helping me make this connection. And I realized that I had to find out more about who my people were and to do my part in telling their story.

Later that summer John, who had been persuaded not to divorce me after all, helped me to contact a Yoruba priest in Brooklyn who specialized in connecting with the ancestors. Baba Abu Bakr was handsome—over six feet tall with smooth caramel skin and dreadlocks that hung down to his waist. Abu was also a musician and an artist who painted brilliantly colored Afro-spiritual canvases of his guardian angels and spirit helpers.

In his youth Abu had lived "African style" with a harem of five wives. Although this arrangement had self-destructed several years earlier, he remained close to his nine grown children. One of his daughters danced with the famous Alvin Ailey Company in New York.

Abu's Fulton Street neighborhood was a tough area, full of hustlers, pimps, gang-bangers, and dope dealers. But the toughest among them respected Abu, and absolutely nobody messed with him. Every day Abu would patrol the streets with Apollo, his attack dog. Apollo stood about four feet high, looked like a small lion, and weighed as much as a good-sized man. Once he got to know you Apollo was fine, but meeting him for the first time could be pretty scary. Whenever he encountered a stranger, Apollo would study them fixedly while emitting a soft, low growl. You could tell that with just one word from his master, the dog would be thrilled to rip both your arms off and eat them for lunch. As I said, nobody messed with Abu.

Despite his fierce demeanor, Baba Abu had a good heart. He could see that my interest in learning more about the ancestors was sincere. After some exploratory meetings, he agreed to teach both John and me.

I began to understand the Yoruba religious system. The Yoruba believe in a form of reincarnation. When a person dies, he reincarnates within his family group. This is why, Abu told me, so many people from the same family will share common characteristics from generation to generation. Our ancestors were in a position to advise and guide us from their broader perspective in the spirit world. It was, therefore, advisable for the living to honor this connection on a regular basis by praying to the ancestors and making small offerings.

The most important thing to understand, Baba Abu taught me, was the universality of the ancestor religion. A relationship with the ancestors was everyone's birthright, regardless of race, creed, or religious belief. All human beings had ancestors, and all human beings could benefit by connecting to them more consciously.

There was no need for me to give up being a Christian. Everyone had ancestors, no matter what their religion. My ancestors—generations of sober, churchgoing Methodists—would never want me to abandon my religion. Honoring my ancestors, or "eguns" as the Yoruba call them, was simply a part of connecting another level of my humanity.

By this time Aunt Marjory's ashes had been sitting in a box on top of my piano for eighteen months while my family tried to decide how to dispose of them. Some family members felt she should be buried with my father and grandparents in the Wilkins family plot in Chicago. Others favored keeping her in a nice urn on someone's mantelpiece. Aunt Marj herself had often expressed the desire that her ashes be scattered around her neighborhood in Brooklyn. In our highly proper and deeply conservative family, the idea of such a thing was quite shocking—which was, I am sure, why Aunt Marj had enjoyed suggesting it.

More time passed. Aunt Marjory's box continued to sit on the piano. From her perch up in Heaven, I hoped she was enjoying my music, but I was beginning to feel she should have a more official resting place.

One day John had a brilliant idea. "Why don't we just take Aunt Marj back to Brooklyn and sprinkle her as she requested? Nobody else seems to have a better idea. This way you are honoring the woman's last wishes."

John and I decided to discuss the matter of Aunt Marj's final resting place with Baba Abu the next time we were in New York. As usual, Abu's answer made perfect sense.

"Bring her back to Brooklyn where she lived for the past seventy years. Bury most of her ashes during my annual ancestor celebration in Prospect Park. Then you can sprinkle the rest around her neighborhood as she requested."

Perfect.

Two months later, with Aunt Marj's ashes in hand, John and I drove down to Brooklyn from our home in Boston. As we inched through the traffic leading to the park's entrance, we passed scores of folks dressed in African garb heading toward the festivities. Inside the park, hundreds more strolled past stalls selling Caribbean food, African shea butter, and beaded jewelry. Street venders squatted on the sidewalk hawking everything from essential oils to bootleg videos.

While a large group of sweating musicians jammed on an eclectic collection of African drums, horns, and guitars, Abu consecrated a small patch of land at the epicenter of the festivities. Hours passed. Then, while the drummers raised up a mighty call to the spirit world and dozens of white-clad priestesses whirled about in ecstatic dance, Abu began digging a hole deep into the earth.

This womblike aperture was a magic nexus point where the usual rules of this world were temporarily suspended. This was a place where, for one night only, a person could speak to their ancestors across time and space. This was the hole that would receive Aunt Marjory's ashes.

One by one, brightly dressed worshippers of all races and religions knelt down in front of the hole and prayed. The sharp smell of frankincense and the deep thudding of the drums transported me to another place and time. Hours ticked on. Finally my turn came. With John at my side, I tipped the box containing Aunt Marj's ashes over and spilled most of her last remains into the hole.

"Well, Aunt Marj, at last you are returning to Brooklyn with appropriate fanfare. There's music, dancing, bright colors, and good food. I know you will be happy here."

As her ashes tumbled in, a spirit of peace descended over me. Though Aunt Marj had left this earth, whenever anyone sang, danced, or drummed here, she would be celebrated.

At the end of the night, Baba Abu appeared in the center of the ritual circle, wearing a heavy wooden mask and a brightly colored raffia skirt. The sweating drummers pounded out a spine-jarring chorus, and the ancestral spirits carried Abu away. His body jerked and twirled, leaped and strutted. The ancestors stayed with him, dancing, prophesying, and healing until the cops turned us all out of the park in the wee hours of the morning.

The next day John and I took the last of Aunt Marjory's ashes back to the block where she had lived on Union Street. "Goodie two-shoes" girl that I was, I was terrified someone would stop us and demand to know what we were doing. I was pretty sure that dumping a dead person's ashes on the city streets would be frowned upon by the authorities. I didn't want any hassles to mar this last ceremony. But I needn't have worried. Our only audience was a pair of druggies nodding in a doorway at the other end of the block. If we had ripped off our clothes and run naked up and down Union Street, no one would have batted an eye.

John and I drove our rented Ford slowly around the block, throwing Aunt Marj's ashes out the window as we drove. Thanks to a brisk wind that day, more of the ashes ended up inside the car than out. Although we had started this mission with our best funereal demeanor, we were doubled up laughing by our third time around the block. Finally John stopped the car in front of her house and unceremoniously upended the box. After nearly two years, my Aunt Marjory had finally been laid to rest.

As soon as I got back home, I set up a small table in my room and covered it in white cloth. On this small altar, I put water in a crystal bowl, a vase of white flowers, and a picture of Aunt Marj. Night after night I sat cross-legged in meditation, seeking some kind of connection.

"Help me, Aunt Marj. Help me to establish a deeper connection to my ancestors and to my own true nature. Help me to find out who I really am. Help me to connect with my roots."

After I had been practicing this routine daily for a couple of months, a voice inside my head barked an irritated response. "Stop whining, Carolyn! Just look in the scrapbooks. They will tell you everything."

Of course! The scrapbooks! The entire history of the family had been sitting right under my nose, moldering away in the basement. I dragged all ten books upstairs and randomly flipped one open.

Each book contained scores of pictures. I recognized some of the people, but many of them were complete strangers to me. Aunt Marj had befriended hundreds of people during her long lifetime, and it seemed she had photographed each and every one of them. Sorority sisters, students, family. There were musicians, people from the neighborhood. Paging through these myriad images from her past, I wondered if I would ever make sense of any of it.

Amid the pictures, taped precariously to a page near the back, were three yellowing newspaper articles from the *New York Times*. I could not recall ever having seen these pages before, not in all the times I had looked through these albums with Aunt Marj.

The first article read, "March 5, 1954, Labor Post Goes to Negro, First of Race in Sub-Cabinet." Below the headline, my grandfather's face beamed out at the camera. With my Uncle John at his side and an American flag in the background, my grandfather stood ready to stride proudly forward into a new, integrated United States.

I read on. "President Eisenhower today nominated J. Ernest Wilkins of Chicago, a Negro attorney, to be Assistant Secretary of Labor in charge of international labor affairs." The article reiterated the fact that my grandfather was the "first member of his race" to hold a subcabinet position. Mr. Wilkins, the article continued, said that "the fact that he was a Negro would be an aid in his work abroad in behalf of the United States Government. He remarked that three-fourths of the world were not white."

My chest swelled with pride. Of course I had known that my grandfather was an Assistant Secretary of Labor. But I guess I hadn't realized what a truly big deal his appointment had been at the time.

The second *Times* article, taped to the opposite page in Aunt Marj's scrapbook, was much smaller. Dated October 25, 1960, its headline read, "Negro's Ouster Denied: Mitchell Assails Accusation of Making Way for Lodge's Son." In it, Secretary of Labor James Mitchell denies an accusation made by the black congressman Charles C. Diggs that my grandfather had been forced out to make way for the son of Henry Cabot Lodge, a prominent New England politician and longtime Eisenhower supporter.

Wow. My grandfather pushed aside to make a job for the son of some well-connected WASP? Barely four years after taking on the job? Why hadn't I ever heard anything about this?

The third article was my grandfather's obituary. I read the article through carefully:

J. ERNEST WILKINS, L.S. AIDE, 64, DIES
Member of Civil Rights Unit Had Been Labor Assistant—Led Methodist Council
WASHINGTON, Jan. 19 (AP)
J. Ernest Wilkins, a member of the Civil Rights Commission, died of a heart attack at his home here today. His age was 64.
Mr. Wilkins was Assistant Secretary of Labor from 1954 to 1958. He resigned last November.
President Eisenhower issued a statement saying of Mr. Wilkins:
"As a former Assistant Secretary of Labor for international labor affairs and as a member of the Civil Rights Commission, Mr. Wilkins was a gifted and dedicated public servant. He contributed much to the public welfare of our country."
Secretary of Labor James P. Mitchell expressed sorrow over Mr. Wilkins' death and said in a statement:
"He was an admired and able public servant. Mr. Wilkins advanced the welfare not only of our country's minority citizens but that of all our citizens."

The article went on to describe his work in the Eisenhower administration in greater detail. The more I read, the more curious I became. What had it been like to be the only black man at the highest level of government back in 1954? My grandfather had been a true racial pioneer, blazing a trail for today's prominent blacks in government. Condi Rice, Colin Powell, and even Barack Obama could all look back to my grandfather as the man who had helped open the door.

The *Times* obit ended with the statement my grandfather had given the press on the day he was appointed to the position of Assistant Secretary of Labor:

"I consider this an honor not to Wilkins individually but to my race in general. I think that this is an answer, more eloquent than anything I could say to those who say that the American Government is not fair to all of its citizens."

J. Ernest Wilkins had broken many barriers during his lifetime. But at what cost? I couldn't help observing that my grandfather died of a sudden heart attack at the relatively young age of sixty-four. And as I reread the obituary, I was struck by the fact that he died less than three months after his controversial resignation.

Had my grandfather really believed that his historic appointment as the first black Assistant Secretary of Labor Secretary demonstrated our government's fairness to all its citizens? If so, it must have been a brutal shock when he was summarily bounced from the job he had accepted in the glare of nationwide publicity barely four years before. Were the accusations true? Had he been forced to resign? If my grandfather had been a white man, would he have been treated in the same manner?

Was my grandfather shafted by the rich and powerful? If so, how did he react? Did he fight back? What did the rest of the family think about all this? From the moment I read those three articles in Aunt Marj's old scrapbook, my grandfather's life became more than ancient history for me. Discovering the truth about the life and death of J. Ernest Wilkins became an obsession.

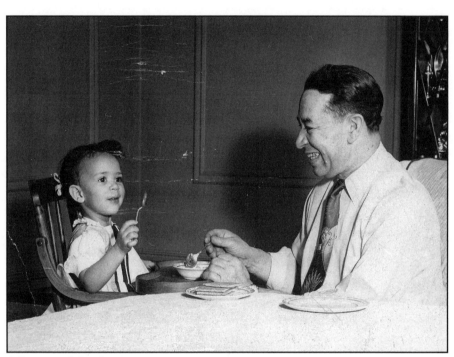

J. Ernest and Carolyn, 1954

Chapter Three

The Early Career of J. Ernest Wilkins

Although my husband, a former librarian, will tell you that contrary to popular belief, everything can not be found on the Internet, a surprising amount of information can be accessed on-line. Using ProQuest's large digital collection of historical newspapers, I was able to download and read scores of articles about J. Ernest Wilkins. A trip to the Boston Public Library yielded more treasures: a biography in *Who's Who,* another biography in *Who's Who in Black America,* and assorted magazine articles from old editions of *Time* and *U.S. News and World Report.* Slowly, a picture of my grandfather's life began to emerge.

The more I found out, the more curious I became. Each nugget of information seemed to lead in a new direction. Books on black history soon began to pile up on my desk and overflow from my bookshelves. After three months of obsessive research, I was overwhelmed. Books and papers filled every corner of my study. The extra chair I kept for visitors had long since become home to a three-foot stack of books and journals. My computer desktop bristled with articles I had downloaded from the Internet. My worktable was covered with scraps of paper on which I had scrawled cryptic notes while reading—"JEW ret F tlk Bkr?"

The trouble was, after a day or two, I couldn't remember where I had put the last cryptic note or just who Bkr was anyway. The only way I was ever going to make any sense of all this information was to compile it into a logical narrative. Just start from the beginning, I thought. Feeling a bit like a high school kid doing her first term paper, I wrote an account of what I had found thus far.

The Early Life of Jesse Ernest Wilkins

J. Ernest Wilkins was born on February 1, 1894, in the town of Farmington, Missouri, which is about sixty miles south of St. Louis. Farmington's high school did not admit black students at the time, so in 1912 my grandfather moved nearly two hundred miles from home to attend Lincoln Institute in Jefferson City, a Missouri state school for blacks founded by African American veterans at the close of the Civil War.[1]

The atmosphere at Lincoln was strict. All students were required to attend a church service every Sunday morning and a religious lecture every Sunday afternoon. Any student foolish enough to curse, gamble, or drink on campus could be expelled instantly.[2] But J. Ernest thrived at Lincoln, and he graduated at the top of his class.[3] After he became successful J. Ernest donated money to the school, and a cash prize was given in his name each year to an outstanding Lincoln graduate. He returned to campus on at least two occasions as a commencement speaker, and again when he was awarded an honorary doctorate from Lincoln in 1941.

When my grandfather graduated from Lincoln in 1914, black students were legally barred from attending the University of Missouri. In order to continue his education J. Ernest was forced to move out of state. In the fall of 1914 he presented his credentials from Lincoln to the registrar at the University of Illinois. Twenty-seven years later, a recording was made of Lincoln's seventy-fifth anniversary Founders' Day Banquet, at which my grandfather told the following story:

> I went to the University of Illinois in nineteen hundred and fourteen and when I presented my credentials there, the Registrar of that University got out a catalogue of the University of Missouri and he looked and he looked and he looked to find Lincoln University on the accredited list of the University of Missouri. I knew what he was doin' but I didn't say anything. He came back and said "Mr. Wilkins what school was that in Missouri you say you came from?" I said Lincoln Institute. He went back and he said, "Mr. Wilkins did you say Lincoln Institute?" I said yes sir. "Well, uh, is that in Missouri?" I said yes sir. He says "well I don't find it listed on the accredited list of the University of Missouri." I can't tell you what I told the registrar, but I started to practicing law then. And before I got through, I had been admitted to the University of Illinois without an examination and without the "OK" of the University of Missouri. I don't know that I could have got it at that time. Certainly I can't get it now. And I say that without any reflection on the University of Missouri because where I come from we hit from the shoulder.[4]

While my grandfather was speaking, the numerous Missouri politicians in the audience must have been squirming in their tuxedos. Only three years earlier, an African American named Lloyd Gaines had tried to enter the University of Missouri Law School. When the school cited the segregation clause in Missouri's state constitution as its reason for rejecting his application, Gaines took the university to court. In 1938 the U.S. Supreme Court ordered Missouri either to admit Gaines or to provide a comparable place for him to study law in his home state. Rather than admit a single black student into its lily-white university, the state of Missouri created a law school at Lincoln for black students.[5] Everyone in the audience that night would have known about the Gaines case.

J. Ernest continued his speech: "We believe in education for everybody. We believe in equal opportunities in the educational field. And if Lincoln University can't give it, the University of Missouri oughta give it!"

If you listen to the recording today, you can feel the energy in the room change as my grandfather speaks. The audience, which had been applauding and laughing along with him just minutes before, now sits silently in their seats, shuffling and coughing. Then, with a bit of deft humor, J. Ernest lightens the mood and introduces the next speaker.[6] It was 1941, not 1971, after all, and he probably felt it would not be expedient or wise to stir up further controversy.

In 1914, my grandfather began his freshman year at the University of Illinois in Urbana, about 150 miles from Chicago. The very fact that the U. of I. admitted black students at all made it the destination of choice for J. Ernest and a handful of other black students from the Midwest. But the atmosphere in town and on campus was hardly welcoming. As late as 1927 black University of Illinois students were being told to "go around back" if they wanted to eat in the city's restaurants. When one black student sued a local eatery for discriminatory treatment, the restaurant owner was found "not guilty" in a matter of minutes by an all-white jury.[7]

Desperate for a way to counteract the isolation and alienation they felt on campus, the university's black students formed their own social group, which they named the Illini Club. In the summer of 1912 a black student at the nearby University of Indiana named Watson Diggs visited the University of Illinois campus. During this visit, he convinced the Illini Club members to join a new organization he had recently created on Indiana University's campus. Diggs called his group the Kappa Alpha Psi fraternity. Founded just the winter before by ten black men at Indiana University's Bloomington campus, Kappa Alpha Psi in its charter proudly proclaimed itself open to membership by college men anywhere, regardless of their color, religion, or national origin.[8]

By the time J. Ernest arrived at the University of Illinois in September 1914, Kappa Alpha Psi's Beta chapter had been in existence for nine months. After passing the required examinations J. Ernest was admitted to the fraternity that same year. For the rest of his life, Kappa Alpha Psi would play an enormous role in my grandfather's life. After he graduated from law school in 1922, J. Ernest became the fraternity's Keeper of Records, a position he held until he was appointed Grand Polemarch (president) of the Kappas in 1947.[9]

Keenly aware that many whites saw African Americans as inferior, the black collegians of my grandfather's era set out to prove that they were not only equal but superior to their white contemporaries. Upon graduation, these students would take their place among the group that NAACP leader W. E. B. Du Bois called the "Talented Tenth." Du Bois hoped this corps of race leaders, through their brilliance and dedication, would lift the black masses out of their second-class status.[10]

This was the philosophy of the time, and the men of Kappa Alpha Psi embraced it with a vengeance. While their white counterparts were having panty raids and guzzling illegal "hooch" at speakeasies, members of Kappa Alpha Psi created mentoring programs for black youngsters and encouraged a high level of academic achievement.[11] For J. Ernest, membership in Kappa Alpha Psi reinforced the core values he had learned at Lincoln Institute: temperance, diligence, rectitude, and service.

Although he had to support himself by working odd jobs after school, J. Ernest excelled at the University of Illinois. Graduating with honors in the field of mathematics, he was a member of the school's mathematics club and was elected to Phi Beta Kappa, the elite society of leaders in intellectual achievement. At this point in his life, J. Ernest's goal was to be a mathematician. But in 1918 the nation was at war. Within weeks of graduation, my grandfather enlisted in the U.S. Army and was assigned to the 809th Pioneer Brigade.

In the early days of the First World War, U.S. Army officials had been reluctant to use black soldiers in combat. Some white officers claimed that black men did not have the courage or the intelligence to fight in battle. Others feared the long-term consequences of putting guns in the hands of an oppressed minority. Once the army finally decided to use black soldiers, they were placed in segregated units and trained at segregated facilities.[12]

In September 1918 the 809th Pioneers were ordered to ship out for France, and they sailed from New York aboard the troop ship *President Grant* with five thousand men on board. During the fourteen-day voyage, over two thousand of these men became infected with a lethal flu virus. The flu epidemic of 1918 traveled back and forth across the ocean on American troop ships, killing more than 20 million people in Europe and America within the next year.[13] Less than three months after graduating from college J. Ernest, far from home and on his first ocean voyage, witnessed the flu's devastating effects firsthand. In the cramped confines of the *President Grant,* the disease spread like wildfire. Young men, who only a few days earlier had been in the pink of health, died by the thousands.[14] There was not even enough room onboard the ship to store all the dead bodies; many soldiers had to be buried at sea, their bodies wrapped in a flag and dumped overboard to disappear forever under the cold grey waves of the North Atlantic. When the ship arrived in France, the 809th Pioneers were assigned the painful task of unloading the remaining bodies of flu victims who had died onboard the ship.[15] Although this traumatic experience must have left a vivid impression, J. Ernest never mentioned it in any of his biographical interviews.

The troops of the 809th Pioneers were stationed in St. Nazaire, France, a central port of arrival for American troop ships. Although they had been trained to fight, the unit's primary function was to build and repair hospitals for the wounded American troops. J. Ernest, a noncommissioned officer, was given the rank of sergeant and put to work in the supply office.[16]

Contrary to the optimistic projections of many black leaders, the thousands of African Americans who volunteered to serve in the U.S. Army were not treated as equals by their white comrades-in-arms. When two French prostitutes in the town of Vannes expressed a preference for black customers, Charles Hamilton Houston, the future dean of Howard University's law school, was nearly lynched by a group of white soldiers. "The officer who led the mob began to yelp about 'niggers' forgetting themselves just because they had a uniform on, and it was time to put a few in their places," Houston later wrote. Many of the college-educated black men who had volunteered for armed service during the First World War returned home disillusioned. Houston explained, "The hate and scorn showered on us Negro officers by our fellow Americans convinced me that there was no sense in my dying for a world ruled by them. My battlefield was America, not France."[17]

By the time he returned to the States in August 1919, J. Ernest Wilkins had chosen a new direction for his life. Although he would always love mathematics, the racial injustice he had experienced as a soldier overseas inspired him to become a lawyer.[18] That fall, my grandfather began his studies at the University of Chicago Law School, supporting himself by working odd jobs and tutoring other students.

It was at the University of Chicago that he met Lucile Robinson. A pert, petite woman with fair skin, wavy hair, and a penetrating intellect, Lucile was studying for her undergraduate degree in mathematics. On a campus with so few black students, it is easy to see how the couple met; they were moving in the same social worlds and shared the same interests. It must have been love at first sight.

Lucile's father, J. W. Robinson, was a distinguished Methodist minister. Tall and handsome with a commanding presence, he presided over a large congregation at Chicago's St. Mark Church on the corner of Fiftieth and Wabash. A charismatic, flamboyant speaker, Robinson told his children that had he not been called to the ministry, he would have become an actor. Robinson's magnetic personality drew hundreds of people from all walks of life to the church. In 1912 Robinson presided over both the funeral of the controversial boxer Jack Johnson's first white wife and his second marriage ceremony three months later to another white woman.[19]

St. Mark Church had an excellent choir, a vibrant youth group, and an invigorating atmosphere. Most of all, however, St. Mark had Lucile Robinson. J. Ernest Wilkins became a lifelong member. No matter how busy he became later in life, my grandfather remained involved in church activities, teaching Sunday school, raising funds for the building committee, and serving as a deacon.

On November 23, 1922, my grandfather and grandmother were married. That same year, J. Ernest graduated from the University of Chicago Law School and passed the Illinois bar exam. Through rigorous self-discipline, intellectual brilliance, and relentless hard work, J. Ernest Wilkins had reached a new pinnacle of personal and professional success.

Compiling this much information had taken months. I now had a better sense of my grandfather's early life and knew about some of obstacles he'd had to overcome on his path to success. But I still did not feel like I knew the man. More important, I still had not found any answers to my major questions. What had happened to my grandfather during his years in the Eisenhower administration? Had he really been forced to resign his position as Assistant Secretary of Labor? Was he a victim of racism? If so, how had he reacted? Within two months of his resignation, J. Ernest suffered a sudden fatal heart attack. Had the stress and disillusionment he experienced during this stormy period killed him?

I had acquired a lot of background information, but to get the real skinny, I was going to have to talk to the people who knew him best. My grandmother Lucile had died in 1964. Two of J. Ernest's sons—my father, Julian, and his brother John—had also passed away. J. Ernest's last surviving son, J. Ernest Jr., was now bedridden and barely able to talk. There were only two family members alive who had known my grandfather well enough to be able to answer my growing list of questions—Uncle John's widow, Constance, and my mother.

In the past, whenever I had tried to talk to Mom about my father's side of the family, she diverted the conversation to other topics. Although she had never gone into details, I got the impression that she didn't really like J. Ernest very much. If I was going to get to the bottom of what really happened to my grandfather back in 1958, I was going to have to find out why.

St. Mark Methodist Church

Chapter Four

Chicago

Although I talk with my mother often by telephone, I don't get back to Chicago to visit as often as I would like. Part of the reason for this is that my mother is an inveterate globetrotter. Even at the age of eighty, Mom will hop on a plane in a heartbeat. She visits my brother David and me in Boston at least twice a year. When my brother Stephen was working as a stockbroker in Thailand, Mom flew over to check out his place in Bangkok. When my brother Timothy's job took him to live in Tokyo, my mother flew over there to visit him. Twice. I, on the other hand, rarely leave home without a compelling reason. The more I tried to unravel the mystery surrounding my grandfather's resignation from the Labor Department, however, the more it seemed that a trip to Chicago would be a good idea.

Sitting with Mom in the kitchen of the three-story townhouse where my brothers and I had grown up, I wondered why I hadn't made the trip sooner. My mother was clearly glad to see me. Although gas was nearly four dollars a gallon, she happily drove me all over the city to see the significant locations in my grandfather's life. She took me past the University of Chicago Law School, where J. Ernest received his law degree. Passing the Gothic buildings that made up the central campus, I imagined Lucile and J. Ernest strolling through the quadrangle on their way to class, or perhaps courting on one of the park benches along the Midway. Twenty years later their oldest son, J. Ernest Jr., would also spend five years at the University of Chicago, never receiving a grade lower than B in any class.[1]

Leaving the campus, Mom and I drove through Washington Park and headed north along Martin Luther King Boulevard past the majestic townhouses where black folks of means had lived in the 1940s. The neighborhood had deteriorated significantly since then, but the gray stone houses still maintained an air of elegance. Turning onto Fiftieth Street, we drove slowly, taking in the sights, before pulling to the curb at the corner of Fiftieth and Wabash. Topped by a small steeple, the building that had once been St. Mark Methodist Church sat on the corner, facing a vacant lot. St. Mark's congregation had long since moved away from the neighborhood, but the building was still being used as a church. Like the rest of the neighborhood it looked somewhat down on its luck, and much smaller than I had imagined.

In the early 1920s when J. Ernest and Lucile were courting, St. Mark had been the place to be. In my mind's eye I pictured what the church would have looked like on the day my grandparents got married. The pews would have been packed with church folk dressed to the nines. There would have been ushers wearing white gloves and black suits to show you to your seat. There would have been women decked out in their finest furs and most outrageous hats. But the thing that would have really set the congregation talking that day was the couple's intellectual brilliance. During a typical wedding ceremony, the minister reads the vows first and then says to the bride, then the groom, "Repeat after me." But J. Ernest and Lucile dispensed with the usual prompting and recited their wedding vows entirely from memory. As they filed out of the church that day, Chicago's black bourgeoisie would have had no doubt that they had just witnessed the union of an extraordinary couple.[2]

My mother's father and Lucile's father had both served at St. Mark during their time as Methodist ministers. When Mom's father led the church for three years in the late 1930s, the family lived around the corner on Fiftieth Street. After gazing at the church for a while, Mom and I went to look for her childhood home. Like many of the other houses on the street, it had been torn down. Only an empty lot now overgrown with weeds and littered with trash marked the spot.

Next, Mom drove me past Provident Hospital, where I was born. When the distinguished black surgeon Daniel Hale Williams had helped to found Provident in 1890, blacks could not always receive service in white hospitals, nor could black doctors easily practice there. In 1952, when I was born, my grandfather was a member of Provident's board of trustees. Mom remembers that J. Ernest arranged for her to have the best possible treatment there, including her own private suite. Although many black hospitals in other cities have closed their doors since the coming of integration, Provident Hospital continues to remain open, a reminder of the clout, wealth, and voting power of Chicago's black community.

Turning south on Cottage Grove Avenue, we crossed under the tracks of the "L" train at Sixty-third Street and made a left on Sixty-seventh Street toward Evans Avenue. The modest three-story brick home where J. Ernest and his family lived for over thirty years sat in the middle of the block on a small lot surrounded by a chain-link fence. Next to the house stood a single-car garage with a long driveway.

As my mother and I pulled up to the curb, I remembered that Daddy had driven my brothers and me past this house a few times when I was a little girl. He'd never really made too much of it. I suppose in his own way, he'd been taking a trip down memory lane, just as I was doing now. Dad had been dead for twenty-four years, but in that moment I missed him terribly. "Here I am, Daddy," I said to myself. "I've come to find out about J. Ernest and about our family."

Mom and I parked and got out of the car.

"Which one was Daddy's room?" I asked her. She pointed to the second floor of the house, where a small dormer window covered by a striped awning over-looked the street. "What's it like inside there?" I asked her. She shrugged.

"It was OK. Not the fanciest house but a nice house. There used to be a little yard with a tree in it around back. I'm going to take a look."

As Mom headed off down the block to inspect the rear of the house, I stood looking up at the small dormer window, thinking about my father.

In the 1930s when my dad was growing up, Chicago's neighborhoods were as segregated as those of any city in the Deep South. At the time, the public schools on the city's predominately black South Side were in terrible shape. Even when compared with the inferior schools reserved for black children in other large northern cities, Chicago public schools fared poorly. My mother had been an "A" student at Farren Elementary School when she lived in Chicago. But when her family moved to New York in 1940, Mom instantly found herself two full grade levels behind the rest of her classmates.

J. Ernest and Lucile knew only too well that a poorly educated black child had little chance of success in life. They were determined not to allow the Chicago public school system to hamstring their children. Powered by the belief that only exceptional people could escape the second-class status meted out to most blacks, J. Ernest and Lucile drove their children relentlessly. My grandparents had been math majors in college. They played math games with their three children at home, even when they were babies, and tutored them in reading. When it was time for the boys to go to school, the Wilkins children bypassed the nearby McCosh School. Instead, they were sent to Willard Elementary, where Lucile worked as a math teacher.

Chicago's segregated public schools were not equipped to handle the intellectual prowess of the Wilkins children. Unable to challenge them intellectually in any meaningful way, teacher after teacher simply skipped the boys on to the next grade. J. Ernest Jr. was the oldest of the three and set the pace for his two younger brothers. Always his father's favorite, J. Ernest Jr. possessed a genius-level IQ, got his PhD at age nineteen, and went on to study with Albert Einstein. John and Julian would have to rise to unusual heights simply to keep up. My father, who graduated from elementary school when he was eleven, was considered the "slow" one in the family.

The three boys competed fiercely among themselves for the approval of their parents. In every contest, no matter how small, everyone's self esteem was on the line. Even as an adult, my father could be brutally competitive. He always played to win and would sulk if he lost at anything, even if it was only a bowling match with us kids.

Only sixteen months apart, my father and John each graduated from Wendell Phillips High School at age fourteen and were enrolled at the University of Wisconsin in Madison one year apart. Looking at the picture of his freshman class, I am struck by how lonely my dad and his brother must have been. The only black students in a sea of strapping white farm boys, Julian and John would have been out of place even if they had been eighteen. I can't even begin to imagine what it must have felt like to have your first collegiate experience at fourteen, at a virtually all-white campus, miles from home. In the picture Julian and John stand in separate rows, frail, somber, and unbelievably young. They may have felt alienated and overwhelmed, but the two Wilkins brothers had each other.

In the pressure-cooker environment of their home, as boys among the college men at Wisconsin, and then as roommates at Harvard Law School, the two brothers stood together against the world. To his dying day, I don't believe there was anyone my father loved more than his brother John. Years later, when a stroke disabled John in San Francisco, my father wrote him every day from Chicago. John's widow, Constance, tells the story that, as kids, John and Julian had a nightly ritual in the room they shared. After the lights went out, one of the boys would throw a shoe at the other. Then the other one would throw it back. Every night for fourteen years—two shoes, two brothers. This was probably the closest they could come to expressing the intense love they felt for each other.[3]

Love was definitely at a premium in the Wilkins household. J. Ernest did not become the phenomenal success he was by going easy on himself in any way. His path had been arduous, and he was well aware of the fine line society drew between success and failure for black men. It was important to be not merely adequate in life but impeccable. Both Aunt Constance and my mother described J. Ernest's criticism of his boys as "unrelenting," "harsh," and "extreme." Even when they had grown to adulthood, J. Ernest rode his boys hard.

When John and Julian joined the family law practice after graduating from Harvard Law School, J. Ernest hectored them frequently. "You just don't think," he would thunder, looking over a brief they had prepared. "What were you thinking!"[4]

Intensely concerned with maintaining the good name and the high regard in which he was held, J. Ernest policed himself and his family ruthlessly for any cracks in their perfect façade. Life was full of pitfalls. One could not be too careful.

"Yep. The yard's still there, but the tree looks awful." Back from her stroll around the block, my mother's voice jolted me out of my reverie.

"What was it like for my dad growing up here?" I asked her.

Mom reflected for a moment. "Lucile and J. Ernest were hard on their children, Carolyn. Your father never felt he was bright enough or good enough to suit either one of them. J. Ernest was very critical. I can't really say much more than that."

While we'd been driving around that afternoon, Mom had regaled me with story after story about her childhood on Fiftieth Street. The time some tough kids threatened to beat her up after school and her big brother Paul had to walk her home. The time she was scratched by a rabid cat from the house next-door and her arm swelled up "as big as a balloon." The time Captain Dyett, who had taught Nat King Cole at DuSable High School, suggested that her brother John learn to play the French horn, starting him on a lifetime career in music.

However, when I asked Mom to tell me stories about my grandfather, she became strangely reticent. My mother is a woman of the "Old School." She would never come straight out and criticize anyone. She had always taught us when we were growing up, "if you can't say anything good, it's best not to say anything at all." I could see she was doing her best to stick to that philosophy.

Later that afternoon, however, as we relaxed over platters of fried chicken and waffles at a South Side eatery, I asked her again about J. Ernest. Maybe it was the homemade gravy, or the candied yams that came as a side dish? Whatever the reason, Mom was now willing to talk about the past.

In December 1950 when my parents got married, my mother had been halfway through her last year of graduate school at Smith College. The wedding had been on Christmas Eve, and the couple had only a few days to spend together before my mom returned to college in Massachusetts. Since J. Ernest and Lucile would be away on vacation for a few weeks, my parents decided to save money. Instead of going to a hotel for their honeymoon, they would stay at my grandparents' home on Evans Avenue. To mark the beginning of his married life, my father had purchased a brand-new bedroom set and installed it in his old bedroom.

My mom recalls that it had been a bitter winter. On the second or third day after the wedding, Chicago was hit by a major snowstorm. Mother was distinctly not pleased when J. Ernest and Lucile called late the following night to announce that they had returned to Chicago several days earlier than anticipated. Mom was even less pleased when J. Ernest and Lucile demanded that my father, honeymoon or no honeymoon, drive to the airport immediately and pick them up.

The exact words spoken between my mother and father upon receiving this summons have been lost to history. But my father was nothing if not a dutiful son. He got up from his honeymoon bed, put on his overcoat and galoshes, shoveled a foot of snow from the driveway, carefully eased the car out of the garage and onto the street, and drove off to Midway Airport to pick up his parents. But he was not quite careful enough. My mother recalls that Dad somehow broke one of the side mirrors on the car that night. And in a voice still shaking with indignation after nearly sixty years, she told me, "And do you know J. Ernest and Lucile made your father pay for the repairs. Can you imagine!"

My grandfather had had to pinch pennies his whole life, working his way through high school, college, and law school and doing whatever odd jobs came his way. Although he had successfully lifted himself into the ranks of the middle class by 1950, money remained important to J. Ernest. His life growing up poor in Farmington, Missouri, had taught him that people who could hold on to their money would have the ability to control their own destiny, while those who threw money away frivolously would have nothing left for a rainy day.

When the army drafted his eldest son and sent him to Tuskegee University to teach pre-flight math to the famous Tuskegee airmen, J. Ernest made sure that Junior sent home a detailed accounting of his daily expenses at the end of every week. Although his son was now a college professor and a grown man with his own paycheck, J. Ernest needed to be sure that Junior was not frittering his money away.[5] J. Ernest believed that those without money were destined to be forever at the beck and call of others. Among his daughters-in-law, my grandfather's cheapness was legendary.

When J. Ernest went to work in Washington in 1954, he and Lucile sold their Evans Avenue home, though the couple continued to spend their vacations in Chicago. According to Mom, they did not want to spend the money it would cost to stay in a hotel. J. Ernest and Lucile expected my parents to put them up for the duration of every visit. Mom recalls one sweltering August in particular, when J. Ernest and Lucile descended on the house and stayed for several weeks. While they were in town, my grandparents' many friends and acquaintances would stop by, and my mother, pregnant with David and with three-year-old me in tow, was expected to entertain the lot.

"Just imagine, Carolyn. There was no air conditioning then. J. Ernest and Lucile would sit in the front room with the windows open getting a nice cool breeze while I was cooking and cleaning in the kitchen, pregnant, and with a three-year-old child!"

"Didn't they ever offer to help?" I asked.

"Not once," Mom replied. "They were the Wilkinses, after all. All of Chicago fawned over them and they felt entitled."

The situation eventually came to a head when J. Ernest, unbeknownst to Lucile, slipped Mom a hundred dollars (a lot of money in 1955) to buy herself a dress. Mom, surprised and pleased, mentioned the gift to Lucile who, my mother remembers, "hit the roof." Whereupon Mom told Lucile that she regarded the couple's summer-long visit as a "serious imposition." Whereupon Lucile reported Mom's remarks to J. Ernest and thus created a major full-blown family brouhaha.

My father, caught between his indignant wife and his domineering mother, refused to take sides. As he would often do when family situations became too emotionally difficult, Dad simply ignored the entire controversy.

"Wilkins men don't stick up for their women," Mom told me, shaking her head. "That's why I had to stick up for myself. If I didn't say something, no one else was going to."

My mother took another bite of fried chicken, her mind still turning over events more than fifty years in the past.

"Lucile was some kind of bigwig on the Methodist women's board, and she was always traveling to conferences and so on. Well, often before she was due to travel, she'd 'get sick.' She'd take to her bed, and I'd have to go out to their house and cook and clean for them. And then, soon as it was time for her to leave, she'd recover miraculously. She'd be out of the house and *gone*. That Lucile. She was some piece of work."

I had known for some time that my mother had not been a big fan of my grandmother. But what I really wanted to know was whether she had ever heard any family discussions about J. Ernest's position at the Labor Department. If it was true that my grandfather had been forced out of his job, perhaps the blow had not come all at once? Perhaps there had been signs? Perhaps J. Ernest had talked things over with his sons, all of whom were adults with successful careers of their own in 1958? I asked Mom about it.

"Oh no," she told me. "He never said a word. Your father and I didn't know a thing about it until J. Ernest was fired."

"He was fired?" I asked her.

"Well, he left, however you want to put it. I found out about it by reading the papers like everyone else."

Maybe Mom was holding out on me? Surely an event of this magnitude would have at least been mentioned around the family dinner table?

"Well, what about after he resigned?" I pressed her. "Didn't anyone in the family talk about it? It must have been a terribly stressful time for him."

"No, Carolyn, I'm telling you. J. Ernest never said a word. And your father never said a word."

"Well, do you think the stress of being forced to resign killed him? You know he died almost three months after his resignation."

"Could be, Carolyn. He'd just come home from a trip the night he died. He was alone, you know. Lucile was away at some conference or other. The neighbors noticed that the lights in his house had been on all night, so they called the police. When the officers arrived, there was J. Ernest dead on the floor, surrounded by open suitcases. He'd had a hemorrhage, and there was blood everywhere. And it was your father who had to make the trip down to Washington in the dead of winter to identify the body."

"And how did Daddy take it?" I asked.

"Well, Carolyn, Wilkins men do not talk about their feelings. He never cried or anything like that. Not at his father's funeral, and not at his mother's either."

The inability to express or cope with emotion seemed to be a trait shared by all three of J. Ernest's sons. There was some kind of emotional disconnect that rendered them incapable of facing their own emotions or the emotions of others. When it came to expressing any kind of emotion, my father had been completely blocked. He had never been able to bear discussion of any personal issues. He was known to walk out in the middle of any conversation that threatened to get even a little emotional. All three of the Wilkins brothers were like that. I began to suspect that perhaps this emotional disconnect was a behavior they had learned from their own father. Although my grandfather was described by the press as "modest," "self-effacing," "unassuming," and "soft spoken," family members who knew him best used different words to describe his personality, words such as "pompous," "punctilious," "humorless," even "cold."

At least in the eyes of his daughters-in-law, J. Ernest had been a tightly self-contained man who was ruthlessly critical of himself and others. Of course, my mother and Aunt Connie were much younger than my grandfather when they knew him. His peers were now long gone, so there was no way to know if J. Ernest had unbent a bit more around people his own age. From what my mom told me, however, this didn't seem likely. Although Chicago's black bourgeoisie lionized J. Ernest he seemed to have had few, if any, confidants.

On my way back to Boston in the plane the following afternoon, I mulled over what I had learned about my grandfather during my Chicago trip. I was still in the dark on the subject of his resignation, but I had acquired some useful insights into his personality. Pulling down the tray table from the back of the seat in front of me, I opened up my diary and began a new list of research questions.

What exactly caused J. Ernest to resign his Labor Department position?

Why had he not told his sons about what he was going through during this crucial period in his life?

Why had he been so emotionally distant, even from the people he loved the most? This inability to address emotional issues was a trait he had passed on to all his sons. Had J. Ernest inherited this emotional disconnect from his own father?

As I wrote out these questions, I realized that in all the profiles, interviews, and bios I had seen so far, J. Ernest had never given his parents more than a cursory mention.

What had J. Ernest's relationship with his own father been like?

As the plane started its descent into Boston's Logan Airport, I remembered a story that Aunt Marjory had told me years ago.

Aunt Marj tells the story of Jeremiah

Chapter Five

I Discover a New Ancestor

As usual, Aunt Marjory and I were looking through one of her scrapbooks.

"Look at this picture, Aunt Marj. My dad as a little boy with his parents. When was this picture taken?"

Aunt Marjory pulled the book closer to her rheumy eyes and touched the picture thoughtfully. The large rhinestone rings she wore on almost every finger sparkled in the dimming light.

"My sister Lucile, her husband, J. Ernest, and Julian, your daddy. All dead now, rest their souls."

"Tell my about my grandfather, Aunt Marjory. I never really knew him. Tell me about his family. What was my great-grandfather like? Do we know anything about him?"

She paused reflectively, took a sip of orange soda, and sat up a little straighter in her chair.

"Your grandfather was the illegitimate son of a big-time white judge in Farmington, Missouri," she told me, grinning impishly at the look of stunned surprise on my face. "You know why he calls himself J. Ernest Wilkins? Because the 'J' stands for Jesse, and that was his father's name. He hated his father, so he swore never to use his name."

As I remembered this story, I had trouble imagining my highly polished and socially accomplished grandfather either as an illegitimate child or as someone who could hate his father enough to change his own name. After the initial shock of her story wore off, I was more than a little skeptical about its veracity. Aunt Marjory was a flamboyant storyteller who had no qualms about making a good story into a better one. However, if what she said was true, it might explain why my grandfather had always pushed himself so hard to succeed. In a small straight-laced town such as Farmington, illegitimacy would have been considered a real scandal, and J. Ernest could well have felt the need to prove himself to town gossips who predicted he would never amount to anything.

I wasn't yet sure what any of this had to do with his resignation from the Labor Department, but it was definitely an interesting lead. After I returned from Chicago, I began to research J. Ernest's early years in Farmington. I spent hours on the Internet, visiting various sites that promised help with ancestor research. I read books on Missouri history, searching for clues. I pored over hundreds of census records, looking for his father, Jesse Ernest Wilkins Sr.

It wasn't long before I ran into a significant problem. Re-reading the biographical sketches I had found in newspaper articles, I saw that when my grandfather referred to his own parents, he gave their names as Henry B. Wilkins and Susie O. Douthit. The "Jesse Ernest Wilkins Sr." that Aunt Marjory had talked about didn't seem to exist. My frustration mounted as I searched for Jesse Ernest Wilkins Sr. on a popular ancestor research site, without success.[1] I couldn't find any connection between my grandfather and either Henry B. Wilkins or Jesse Ernest Wilkins Sr. Had there been some misprint in my grandfather's biography? Had Aunt Marjory gotten her names mixed up?

Perhaps my grandfather's birth certificate would correctly list his father's name? I called the courthouse in Farmington to inquire. A woman from the county clerk's office informed me that no official records of births in that part of Missouri were kept until 1910.

I was now at a standstill and completely frustrated. I would probably have abandoned the search altogether if my husband, John, hadn't stepped in. John is a former librarian. While I tend to be impatient by nature, always looking toward the final outcome, John is a more "details" kind of a person. One morning as I was bemoaning my latest research fiasco over breakfast, John interrupted me. "Carolyn, you don't have the skills, the time, or the personality for this kind of work. There are lots of professional researchers available. Why don't you just hire somebody?"

As usual, John was right.

Within a few days I was in touch with a woman named Mariah Cooper who specialized in ancestor research. After checking her references, I sent Mariah the bare facts I had amassed about my grandfather: when and where he was born, when and where he died, his mother's name, the two possible names of his father. For good measure I also sent her some information about Aunt Marjory's parents. Aunt Marj had always said we came from Africa. Maybe my new researcher would be able to trace our family back to its roots?

Weeks passed. I taught my students. I played the piano and performed with my jazz group. And I waited for the mail every day with the excited anticipation of a kid on Christmas morning.

A short time later, Mariah's package arrived. Inside a large manila envelope I found a short note and some newspaper clippings.

"There is no Jesse Wilkins in Farmington," Mariah's letter read. "Your great-grandfather's legal name was John Bird Wilkins, and he was an African American. What's more, he seems to have been a Baptist minister. Enclosed are some newspaper articles about him that I found."

I read and re-read her letter in amazement. Not only was Aunt Marj's story completely off base, even my grandfather's biographers in *Who's Who* seemed to have gotten their basic facts wrong. When I shared my discovery with other family members, they were equally flummoxed. No one, not even older relatives who had known my grandfather well, had ever heard of John Bird Wilkins.

With Mariah Cooper's expert help, I spent the next few weeks attempting to unearth more information about John Bird. But despite our hours of diligent research, concrete information about my great-grandfather proved difficult to come by. As the weeks devoted to my research stretched into months, it became clear that John Bird Wilkins had been a flagrant liar throughout his whole lifetime, deliberately obscuring significant facts about his past.

If I had been curious about my great-grandfather before I discovered his mendacious ways, I was now thoroughly fascinated. Though he was best known as a Baptist minister, John Bird Wilkins was also a teacher, an inventor, and a newspaperman who led a complex (and bigamous) personal life. He was married and became a widower in Mississippi when he was in his twenties. In the late 1800s, John Bird maintained simultaneous common law relationships with two Farmington women. From these alliances, he fathered seventeen children, one of which was my grandfather.

Perhaps because of his complicated marital situation, my great-grandfather used a number of different aliases. Sometimes he called himself Bird J. Wilkins, Reverend Bird J. Wilkins, even Bishop Bird J. Wilkins. On other occasions, he went by Howard Wilkins or H. B. Wilkins, or Reverend H. B. Wilkins, as the situation required.

In a 1927 interview with a reporter from the *Chicago Defender*, John Bird called himself "Dr. J. B. Wilkins." At this time he claimed to have graduated from Rochester Theological Seminary, Jefferson Medical College, and Harvard. He also said that he was a psychoanalyst, and that Clarence Darrow had consulted him in "a recent Chicago criminal case."[2]

These statements impressed me, until I realized that my great-grandfather had given himself a new resume for each of his newspaper interviews. He told the *Chicago Tribune* he had studied theology at Hamilton College.[3] Six months later he told the same paper he had attended Hamilton College but had studied his theology at Shaw University.[4] Later still, John Bird would tell a reporter from the *Chicago Defender* he had attended Rochester Theological Seminary, Jefferson Medical College, and was the third black student to graduate from Harvard.[5]

When my great-grandfather died, two conflicting obituaries gave information about his life. The *Chicago Defender* reported that he "was a friend of Fredrick Douglass whom he met while attending Howard University" and that he had "worked his way through school while in the employ" of the distinguished journalist Horace Greeley. His obituary in the *St. Louis Argus* reported that my great-grandfather had gone to Gammon Theological Seminary and to Yale.[6]

After months of diligent checking and cross-checking, I could not find evidence that substantiated any of these claims. Even John Bird Wilkins's place of birth is in doubt. Although he claimed to have been born in Nashville, Tennessee, the various federal census entries under his name list different birth states at different times—Tennessee, Georgia, and Mississippi are all possibilities. The only thing I could determine with any certainty about my great-grandfather's origins is that he was born in the South sometime between 1849 and 1856. When asked about his early life by a reporter for the *Chicago Defender* in 1927, John Bird described himself as having been "a slave, motherless soon after birth, and, under the conditions of those evil days, also fatherless," who was "sold down the river" as a young boy.[7]

A detailed search of the federal census records indicates that my great-grandfather's traceable story most likely begins in Oxford, Mississippi. On July 18, 1870, five years after the end of the Civil War, the Lafayette County census marshal interviewed a young farm laborer named J. B. Wilkins. In this census, Wilkins is described as a "mulatto," that is, light-skinned, possibly of mixed white and black parentage. He lives near Oxford, Mississippi, with his twenty-one-year-old brother, William, and his younger siblings, Leroy, Mary, and Jesse (for whom my grandfather is most likely named). John Bird's brother William cannot read or write and works as a laborer.[8]

Even as a young man, however, John Bird seems to have eluded any attempt to pin him down definitively to any one place or time. Six weeks after J.B.'s census interview, the Lafayette County census taker finds a mulatto schoolteacher named John Wilkins boarding with a family named Anderson.[9] Is this John Wilkins also my great-grandfather? It seems likely. Traveling conditions in those days were difficult and a journey of even a few miles could take a full day on foot. Perhaps John chose to leave his family in order to live closer to wherever he was teaching.

There is another man named Wilkins living in the Oxford area at this time. His name is William H. Wilkins. He is a white man and a pillar in the local community. Fifty years later, his great-granddaughter Sally would become a playmate and confidante of Oxford's favorite son, the novelist William Faulkner.[10]

This Wilkins, a minister at the local Cumberland Presbyterian Church, counted five slaves among his possessions in 1860, including two boys, aged eleven and five years old. According to the 1860 census, Washington Porter Wilkins, the good reverend's son, made his living as a "Negro trader."[11] Was Washington Wilkins the slaver who brought young John Bird "downriver" to Oxford? Are my great-grandfather and his brother William the two boys W. H. Wilkins owned in 1860? The evidence is circumstantial and highly speculative, but the story is possible.

For years I had been searching for my ancestors and wondering what their lives might have been like. As I contemplated my great-grandfather's life, I was at last coming face-to-face with the sordid realities of slavery, not as something out of a dusty history book but as an intimate family experience. What would life have been like for a slave living around Oxford in 1860?

On the local genealogy Web site, Lafayette County historian Evelyn Crocker directed the following comments to "Our African American Citizens" seeking information about their slave ancestors: "I have found in my research that most of their people were treated kindly by their masters, as kindly as most masters treated their own children and wives when they were obedient to his wishes. The Planter was head of the household or God Head therefore everyone in his household had to obey his law which was based on religious teaching or receive some type of punishment."[12] Muttering a string of curse words under my breath, I checked the date of Crocker's posting. Perhaps Ms. Crocker had written about the "kindly" treatment meted out to Lafayette County's black slaves sometime in the 1800s? But no. The site had been updated as recently as 2008.

In his book *Faulkner's County: The Historical Roots of Yoknapatawpha,* historian Don H. Doyle offered me a different perspective: "In Mississippi most of the conditions shaping slavery were at odds with the mentality and practice of paternalism."[13] Part of the reason for the harsher nature of slavery in Mississippi, Doyle contended, was that the state was on the western frontier of the slaveholding South. Many Lafayette County farmers were relatively new settlers, fueled by the same fierce ambition that inspired their counterparts to hit the wagon trails of the American West. Lafayette County's planters were in a hurry to make their fortune and had few scruples about how they treated their slaves in order to do so.

The nearest major slave market would have been in Memphis, where future Confederate general and Ku Klux Klan (KKK) founder Nathan B. Forrest ran a thriving "trading camp." This is where many of Lafayette County's slaves were purchased.[14] As a dealer in human flesh, Rev. William H. Wilkins's son Washington would have visited this place often.

Years later, freedman Horatio J. Eden remembers his experience on the auction block at Forrest's slave market: "We were brought out and paraded two or three around a circular brick walk in the center of the stockade. The buyers would stand nearby and inspect us as we went by, stop us and examine us. Our teeth and limbs."[15] It is likely that my great-grandfather, a young boy being sold "downriver," also ran this terrifying gauntlet as a child.

After paying for his slaves, Washington Wilkins would then have chained his purchases together in long lines called "coffles." He would have put hand-cuffs and iron neck collars on the men and fastened the women to each other by tying a rope halter around each of their necks. Joined together by these chains, Wilkins's barefoot slaves would have walked for weeks through the rugged northern Mississippi hill country before arriving at their new homes in Lafayette County.[16] After being torn from his mother and sold on the auction block, my great-grandfather would have made this terrible journey as a small boy. Once the slaves were settled with their new owners, they were subjected to grueling physical labor and harsh discipline. Notwithstanding Ms. Crocker's statement on the genealogical Web site, it has been well documented that the "punishment" these "kind" masters meted out to "disobedient" slaves routinely included whipping, mutilation, or being sold away from their families.[17]

The deeper I delved into the harsh realities of slavery, the more emotionally draining my research became. Just contemplating the fact that I could wake up each morning as a free human being, in relative control of my own destiny, had become enough to send me into paroxysms of weepy gratitude. After a day spent reading books about slavery, I found it difficult to offer sympathy when friends complained about being stuck in traffic or having had a tough day at work.

For weeks after reading them, the words of the former slaves haunted my dreams. Lucindy Shaw, enslaved as a child on a Lafayette County plantation, remembers a life of unremitting hard work: "I had to work mity hard; I had to plow in the fields in the day and den at nite when I wuz so tired I cund't hardly stan' I had to spin my cut of cotton befo' I cu'd go to sleep." During her time on the plantation, Lucindy saw a pregnant woman whipped to death. As the woman's lifeless body was untied from the whipping post, an older slave was told to dig a shallow grave. According to Lucindy, "hit wuzn't nuthin' but a hole in de groun'; he tok the shovel an' jus rolled her in. An' den he shoveled in sunthin' dat I tho't I saw move." The woman had been whipped so hard that she had given birth.[18]

When Lafayette County slave owner J. D. Tankersley killed a female slave in the fall of 1864, he defended himself to his Presbyterian congregation by saying that the slaves had become "unmanageable, rude and insolent, setting at defiance all authority." The church deacons apparently agreed that the young man's actions were justified. Tankersley was officially forgiven for the slave's murder and allowed to remain a member of the church in good standing.[19]

The more I read, the more time I found I needed to spend at the meditation table I had built to honor my ancestors. Now that I was learning about some of what they went through, my admiration for their fortitude and perseverance turned to awe. There was no room for whining or self-pity in this life. Their stories whispered to me, "You are free and have the ability to do whatever you want with your life. Let nothing stand in your way."

In every state in the South, it was against the law for slaves to learn to read. As early as 1823, the Mississippi legislature passed a law mandating a punishment of thirty-nine lashes for anyone caught educating the slaves. A slave anywhere in the South who tried to become literate faced the very real possibility of being beaten, whipped, mutilated, sold, or even hanged.[20] Given this policy of enforced ignorance, it comes as no surprise that in 1870, just six years after Emancipation, the vast majority of Lafayette County's African Americans could neither read nor write.

John Bird, however, had ended up a highly literate and articulate man with wide-ranging and sophisticated opinions on the intellectual issues of his day. From his first appearance in the 1870 census, he is listed as being able to read and write. Exactly how my great-grandfather acquired his education remains a mystery. In his 1927 interview with the *Chicago Defender*, John Bird maintained that he had been taken up to Boston by a Miss Webb from the Freedman's Bureau and eventually continued his studies at Harvard.[21]

Although there was an Emma Webster teaching at a school for freedmen in Oxford after the Civil War, there is no indication that she was from Boston. John Roebuck, a former Confederate soldier, writes of a "high toned, philanthropic 'lady'" who came to teach in southern Lafayette County "from the slums of some Northern city." But this woman was able to remain in the area for only three weeks before the local whites threatened to tar and feather her. Roebuck reports that, fearing for her life, the teacher left Lafayette County immediately and never returned.[22] Perhaps this woman is the schoolteacher to whom my great-grandfather refers. It's unlikely she took him to Boston, however, since the 1870 census places John Bird in Oxford for at least part of that year.

Oxford, after all, was no ordinary Mississippi town. By naming it after the famous English University, Oxford's founding fathers had made their intentions for the town clear. Oxford was to be a center of learning and culture, a beacon of civilization on the Mississippi frontier. The state's largest educational institution, the University of Mississippi, was located in Oxford. In the 1860s Oxford was also home to North Mississippi College and Union Female College, where Rev. W. H. Wilkins served as a steward in 1844.[23] As one of Wilkins's five slaves, my great-grandfather would have grown up in proximity to many educated people, including several teachers. As a whole, Oxford's ministers seemed to have taken a more liberal approach to the issue of black literacy than many

Mississippi planters. Hugh Barr, a slave owner and Presbyterian deacon, held weekly reading classes for all his slaves.[24] Cumberland Presbyterian ministers S. G. Burney and James Waddell worked actively to create a Sunday school for the education of Oxford's freedmen at the end of the Civil War.[25] Although W. H. Wilkins was a slave owner and a staunch supporter of the Confederacy, it seems likely that someone in his family taught my great-grandfather how to read.

In both of J. B. Wilkins's census entries, he is described as "mulatto," while his older brother, William, is described as "black." My great-grandfather would later claim to be from the "English" Napier family, a wealthy and influential Scotch family in Nashville.[26] One of Nashville's most prominent black citizens in the early 1900s, William Carroll Napier, was a descendant of this family. Though there is no evidence that J. B. Wilkins was in any way related either to this man or to the Napier family, there was certainly a white ancestor somewhere in my great-grandfather's very recent past. A drawing made of John Bird Wilkins in 1886 shows him to be a handsome, fair-skinned man with an aquiline nose and long wavy hair.

As I pondered this information, I was once again brought back to the issue of skin color. As hard as I tried to avoid it, the time had come for me to address the question of how my great-grandfather came by his light skin and Caucasian features. According to historian Don H. Doyle, between one-third and one-fifth of the adult white males in Lafayette County did not have a white female counterpart, circumstances creating what he called "a situation rife with temptation for sexual exploitation and clandestine interracial unions."[27] There was an eighteen-year-old female slave living in W. H. Wilkins's household around the time my great-grandfather was born. Perhaps John Bird was not brought into Mississippi from Tennessee as he told reporters in 1927. Perhaps, instead, my great-grandfather's birth was the result of an interracial alliance between this slave and someone in the Wilkins family?

Truth was, thinking about this whole subject made me uneasy. All my life I had fought hard to be seen as "authentically" black. I was distinctly underwhelmed at the thought that my great-grandfather may have been the unacknowledged progeny of some philandering slaveholder. When I mentioned the subject to my husband, John, he added fuel to the fire by pointing out that Wilkins's slave-trading son Washington would have been a teenager at the time my great-grandfather was conceived. "Great!" I told him sarcastically. "Just what I always wanted, a slaver in the family tree."

After John's continued teasing over my family's ironic Faulknerian connection provoked a nasty marital argument, we both agreed to table the subject. But of course I still thought about it. If this is the way my great-grandfather had come into the world, perhaps it explained his unwillingness to tell the truth about his background. If John Bird was, in fact, an unacknowledged relative of the white Wilkins family, perhaps this explains why he was taught to read while his darker brother, William, was not.

If he is the "John Wilkins" listed in the census for that year, my great-grandfather was working as a schoolteacher by 1870. Oxford's first school for freedmen had opened in 1866. The school's founder, a courageous black minister named Alexander Phillips, had been subjected to a nightmarish campaign of harassment and intimidation by the KKK. After Phillips was shot in the head by a drunken white man, federal troops garrisoned nearby had been called in to restore order.[28]

It's quite possible that John Bird began his career as a teacher at Phillips's school, though, as usual, there is little concrete information to go by. If the thought of being shot by hostile whites intimidated my great-grandfather, he never mentioned it. In an interview for the *Chicago Tribune* years later, John Bird would speak proudly of having moved his classroom outdoors after his schoolhouse was torched by the KKK.[29]

John Bird refers to this incident as having occurred in South Carolina, but I could find no record of his ever having lived in that state. Ten miles outside of Oxford, however, Daniel Perkins Borum, a white man from South Carolina, did attempt to open a school for blacks. After local planters complained that "their" blacks were leaving their work in the fields to attend classes, Borum's school was indeed burned to the ground. When teachers showed up for work the next day, they found a notice beside the smoking ruins, warning against any future efforts at educating the freedmen.[30]

The early 1870s were a time of violence, chaos, and new beginnings for the town of Oxford. While many whites saw gloom in the changes wrought by the Civil War, African Americans viewed the Reconstruction period as a time of unparalleled opportunity. Black men now had the right to vote, to get an education, and to receive a fair wage for their labor. If a man was tired of the low pay and backbreaking grind of plantation work, nothing prevented him from going into the city to look for a better job. At the close of the Civil War, thousands of black men, women, and children hit the road to search for lost family members, for better employment, or just for the sheer exhilaration of being able to travel when and wherever they wanted. Sometime between 1870 and 1873, John Bird Wilkins joined the tide of migrants and moved eighty miles up the road to Memphis.

Left to right: Ernest Jr., John, Julian, J. Ernest, c. 1941

Chapter Six

Memphis, Tennessee, 1874–1878

I am a jazz musician. When I think of Memphis, I think of Beale Street, the blues, and W. C. Handy. As I continued to trace my great-grandfather's story, I realized that while he was alive, Memphis was famous not for its music but for its boomtown status as the fastest growing city in the South.

On February 1, 1873, John B. Wilkins opened an account at the Memphis branch of the Freedman's Bank, located in the heart of the black district on Beale Street. In a clear, bold hand, he gives his address as "Carolina Street" and his occupation as "school teacher."[1]

I imagine Memphis would have impressed my great-grandfather as he strolled along its crowded streets. Home to the nation's largest inland cotton market, the city had a population of over forty thousand, nearly double that of Atlanta or Nashville. Memphis was now the leading producer of cottonseed oil in the nation. Its cotton presses operated twenty-four hours a day, and smoke from its many factories darkened the sky.[2] On the city's crowded streets, scores of wagons laden with merchandise competed for space with horse-drawn carriages, while the sidewalks swarmed with pedestrians.

Along the bluffs overlooking the Mississippi River, new factories and cotton mills seemed to spring up overnight. The din from all the construction must have been deafening. In the first six years following the Civil War, one Memphis firm put up more than 130 new homes, churches, stores, and public buildings around the city. In 1870 plantations in the Mississippi Delta sent more than three hundred thousand bales of cotton upriver to the city's bustling docks, where four railroads and eleven steamship companies waited to carry its cotton products to markets around the world.[3]

African Americans looking for work poured into Memphis and found employment as clerks, mill hands, craftsmen, teamsters, and laborers. Beale Street, on the southern edge of the downtown business district, soon became a focus point for black entrepreneurs. Between 1866 and 1874, twenty black-owned businesses flourished there.[4] For many of the city's new African Americans residents, once they had found a job and a place to live, becoming literate was the next priority. In the city's booming economy, an educated freedman had a host of new opportunities available to him while an illiterate black man could only hope for work as a laborer.

Some Memphis residents, however, did not believe blacks should have access to educational facilities. In 1866 Memphis's whites had rioted and burned the black business district to the ground, killing forty-six people. When the federal government convened a tribunal to investigate the killings, the panel found that "the most intense and unjustifiable prejudice on the part of the people of Memphis seems to have been arrayed against teachers of colored schools."[5]

I am a teacher myself. When I read about the determination and courage with which African American teachers in those days pursued their vocation, I am humbled. What it must have taken for my great-grandfather to get up every day and teach, in the face of the threat of imminent violence and possible death, I can't even begin to imagine.

For those with the fortitude to undertake the challenge, however, there was no shortage of work. Black folks coming out of slavery were hungry for knowledge. Many of these people had spent their entire lives stooped over in fields, digging and chopping. Now they were free, they saw no reason why their children should suffer the same fate. While community leaders begged the authorities to open more schools, whole families squeezed into the city's already overcrowded classrooms.[6]

No matter what his educational background might have been, J. B. Wilkins would have had no trouble finding employment as a schoolteacher in Memphis. Academic credentials, although helpful in securing a teaching position, were not always required. The need was pressing, and black teachers were in short supply. According to historian James Garner, prospective teachers were "asked a few oral questions by the superintendent in his private office, and the certificate was granted as a matter of course."[7]

Working conditions would not have been easy for my great-grandfather as a newly minted schoolteacher. White landowners frequently refused to rent or sell space to African Americans, which forced black schools to meet in private homes and church basements. Even when classroom space was available, the new schools often lacked desks, seats, blackboards, and books. In some classrooms three students might be asked to share a single book, while in others the King James Bible was the only textbook available. Schoolhouses were poorly heated, and many students came to class hungry and in rags.[8]

In their overcrowded classrooms, black teachers often struggled to maintain order. Corporal punishment was the norm. Discipline strategies that would be legally actionable nowadays were considered proper during John Bird's time. Students who neglected their schoolwork, who were tardy, or who talked in class could expect to receive a beating.[9]

Despite the difficulties inherent in his work, my great-grandfather remained in Memphis at least through the spring of 1878, when his name appears in the city directory as "John B. Wilkins (colored), teacher, r 57 Eliott."[10] In the summer of 1874, he returned to the Freedman's Bank to make another deposit, this time as the secretary of his Masonic lodge, King Solomon Lodge Number Two.[11]

Founded in 1784 by Prince Hall, a charismatic former slave from Barbados, the Prince Hall Grand Lodge of Free and Accepted Masons is the oldest black fraternal organization in America. An ambitious Mason in my great-grandfather's day could easily parlay his lodge membership into a network of valuable contacts around the country.[12] John Bird Wilkins seems to have done just that, making connections with Masons from as far away as Vicksburg, Mississippi, and Farmington, Missouri.

As the summer of 1874 began, the future was looking bright. The city of Memphis was enjoying a period of unparalleled prosperity. My great-grandfather had a job, a social network, and two bank accounts. Despite all appearances, however, hard times lay in wait.

Along with thousands of other African Americans, my great-grandfather had deposited his life savings into the Freedman's Bank. Established by an act of Congress in 1865, the bank had been designed to help former slaves acquire the financial skills needed to function in a capitalist economy. If a freedman made a daily deposit of ten cents, he would receive a 6 percent interest on his investment; after ten years his dime-a-day deposit would have grown to $439.31. The nation's African Americans responded enthusiastically to the program, and by the time that J. B. Wilkins opened his first bank account, blacks had deposited over $60,000 into the bank's Memphis branch.[13]

At first, the Freedman's Bank invested its funds in government-backed securities, but in 1870 Congress allowed the bank's directors to speculate in the open market. The bank's financial position began to worsen, and a sudden downturn in the stock market forced bank closings across the country. In a last-ditch effort to shore up its plummeting credibility, the great abolitionist Frederick Douglass was enlisted to serve as the bank's president.[14]

But it was too late. In June 1874 the economy of the entire country spiraled into a depression. The Freedman's Bank, already standing on shaky financial ground, collapsed. And my great-grandfather, like thousands of other African American investors, lost everything.

Boom times were over for Memphis. In August 1878 a major yellow fever epidemic swept through the city killing thousands, white and black alike. "Yellow Jack," as the disease was called, spread rapidly when infected blood was passed through the bite of the *Aedes aegypti* mosquito. Once infected, victims suffered horribly, convulsing in gruesome spasms while they vomited up a thick bile blackened with their own dried blood. There was no cure for the disease; within three days, unless he or she was extremely lucky, the patient would be dead.

By the middle of September, the death rate in Memphis had reached two hundred people a day. Those who could leave the city did so, fleeing in panic-stricken droves. All commercial activity ground to a halt, the factories and cotton mills shut their doors, even the municipal government closed down. By the time the epidemic had run its course in mid-October, the city was nearly deserted.[15]

At some point between 1878 and 1879, my great-grandfather also left town, perhaps to court an Oxford girl named Susie Frierson, whom he married in April 1879.[16] After her marriage to my great-grandfather, Susie Frierson disappears from the record books. After many hours searching records on an ancestry Web site, my researcher Mariah Cooper was unable to find any further trace of her.[17]

In the summer of 1879, on the other hand, a woman named Winnie Jamison in nearby Itawamba County gave birth to John Bird's son, naming the boy Leroy, perhaps after John Bird's younger brother.[18] Even as a young man, it seems, John Bird displayed a taste for bigamy. Did Susie find out about John Bird's other woman and leave him? As usual, a close investigation of my great-grandfather's life seems to generate more questions than answers.

According to the *Record of Educable Children* for Lafayette County, Mississippi, an eleven-year-old boy named John Wilkins and his eight-year-old sister, Mary, attended school in the Town of Oxford during 1885. Their father's name is not given, but their guardian is listed as William Frierson, a blacksmith and prominent citizen in Oxford's black community. Was William Frierson related to Susie? It seems likely. Are these my great-grandfather's children? It certainly seems possible, but I could find no further mention of them, in Oxford or elsewhere, after 1885.

By the summer of 1880, my great-grandfather is listed in the census as widower, once again living with his older brother, William. Although he may have been teaching school at this time, his occupation, at least according to the 1880 census, is that of a laborer.[19] The fate of Leroy's mother Winnie Jamison is also a mystery. Although Itawamba County documents show that my great-grandfather married her in 1881, I could find no further record of her after that date. Black women during this period frequently died young, their lives cut short by malnutrition, disease, or childbirth.[20]

Reading over the information I had compiled about my great-grandfather's life, I was struck by how much violence he must have witnessed. How had this affected his character? Therapists today consider a child to have been traumatized if he experiences even one violent incident during his formative years. My great-grandfather's life to this point would have been one long trauma. Abandoned and sold as a child, enslaved as an adolescent, and twice widowed as a young man, he lived during one of the most chaotic and violent epochs in American history. In 1880, life for a black man in Mississippi was often short and brutal. The more I thought about it, the more impressed I was that John Bird Wilkins had been able to survive at all.

Left to right: Timothy, David, Mom, and Stephen, 2008

Chapter Seven

The Renegade Baptist, 1885–1887

What my great-grandfather did and where he lived between 1880 and early 1885 is a mystery. Knowing that he ultimately became a Baptist preacher, I spent hours in the Boston Public Library searching for his name in the many rolls of microfilm documenting the early history of African American Baptists. I studied newspaper accounts of tent revivals and prayer meetings and foraged in archives hoping to find some reference to him. I had no luck. Later he would claim to have performed over eight thousand baptisms and to have officiated at fifteen hundred weddings.[1] But John Bird Wilkins's name does not appear in any of the many histories written about the black Baptists of this period. He doesn't appear in Patrick Thompson's 575-page *History of the Negro Baptists in Mississippi,* or in Reverend J. A. Whitted's *History of the Negro Baptists of North Carolina.* His name is not among the many ministers profiled in William Hicks's encyclopedic *History of Louisiana Negro Baptists from 1804 to 1914.*[2]

When I was next able to pick up his trail, my great-grandfather was working, not as a minister but as a teacher, in the town of Farmington, Missouri. Located about sixty miles south of St. Louis along the trade route between Missouri's lead-mining region and the Mississippi River, Farmington was a major station on the Iron Mountain Railway. Although the town is nearly three hundred miles from John Bird's last known residence in Oxford, Mississippi, trains ran regularly between Memphis and St. Louis.

Unlike many areas of the Midwest, Missouri had a significant African American population. Although their state had remained in the Union during the Civil War, Missourians had also owned slaves; racial segregation was enforced both by custom and by law throughout the state. Blacks were not welcome at Farmington's white churches, lodges, schools, or community organizations, so they formed their own organizations, built their own churches, and ran their own schools.[3]

In 1870 the city of Farmington erected its first public school. But the new building, by state law, was to be used only by white students.[4] This lack of dedicated classroom space might have presented a challenge to an inexperienced teacher, but John Bird Wilkins, when he arrived in Farmington sometime around 1884, was no longer a newcomer to the teaching profession. Nor, apparently, was he a newcomer to grassroots organizing. Within months of relocating to Farmington, my great-grandfather emerged as a community leader, remembered by his contemporary J. W. Cayce as being "the most efficient school teacher that has ever been in our midst."[5]

On January 12, 1885, Wilkins organized a group called the Colored Working Men's Association to build a gathering place for Farmington's African American community. Under his leadership, money for the project was raised. Every member of the organization was required to pay dues. The Working Men's Association held fund-raising picnics, sponsored festivals, and sent letters to community members asking for contributions. Even civic-minded citizens from Farmington's white community gave money to the project.[6]

Construction on the new hall began in the winter of 1885.[7] Upon completion the building, commonly known as Colored Hall, became an all-purpose home for several of Farmington's black social organizations. Parties, graduations, meetings, and other major community events were held there. St. Paul's Church met there. Later St. Luke's African Methodist Episcopal Church also used the building. The Prince Hall Masons and the Black Knights of Pythias held their initiations upstairs and their large meetings downstairs.[8] Before the two-room schoolhouse on Douglas Street was built, the hall also served as a schoolhouse for black students.[9]

And I imagine that it was here in Colored Hall, perhaps during a lodge event or a church social that my great-grandfather, now calling himself Professor Bird J. Wilkins, first met Susie Douthit. The Douthits lived an easy walk from Colored Hall, not too far from Ethelean Cayce. Susie's parents had married immediately after the Civil War and had six children. Hilliard Douthit, who worked in a sawmill to support his family, was a prominent figure in Farmington's black community and in the 1870s had helped to found St. Paul's Church.[10] Douthit was active in the Prince Hall Masons, so it is likely that he and my great-grandfather attended lodge meetings together.[11]

In 1885, John Bird Wilkins was around thirty-five years old, and single. Contemporary accounts describe him as a charismatic speaker with a pleasing voice and an arresting gaze.[12] He was a slender man with fair skin, a full head of dark wavy hair, and a handlebar mustache.[13] I imagine that many women would have found him attractive.

I wish I had a picture of Susie Douthit. I'd like to imagine my great-grandmother as the town beauty. Fifty years after her death, my Uncle Ernest described her as being a "petite brown-skinned woman." What I do know for sure is that Susie was Hilliard Douthit's baby girl, and she was only seventeen when she met my great-grandfather. Although she could read and write, Susie had probably never been outside of Farmington in her entire life. I can easily imagine that she was swept off her feet by my handsome, and well-traveled, great-grandfather. Where, or if, she and John Bird were married remains a mystery. A diligent search yielded no record of their marriage in any of the states where they lived.

By the summer of 1885 the couple had left Farmington and given birth to their first child. And "Professor" Bird J. Wilkins had not only created a brand-new family, he had also created a brand-new career for himself. "Professor" Wilkins had become "Reverend" Bird J. Wilkins, Baptist minister.

I had always known that there were a lot of ministers in my family. Aunt Marjory and my mother had each told me stories about their respective fathers, both distinguished Methodist clergymen. But a Baptist in the family? Back when I was a kid, I remember Aunt Marj teaching me to sing the following ditty: "I'm a Methodist born, I'm a Methodist bred. When you put me in the ground, I'll be a Methodist dead. Hallelujah, Praise the Lord!" To find we had a Baptist in the family was definitely a whole new concept.

As a musician I've played for synagogues, mosques, Buddhist meditation groups, and Christian denominations of all stripes. What would a service at my great-grandfather's church have been like? Was John Bird a majestic, scholarly speaker? Or did he have a more dramatic preaching style? Did he ever "get the Spirit," dance a holy dance, or speak in tongues? Perhaps my attraction to the sacred trance aspects of African religion had a closer genetic source than I had previously imagined. For years I had sought a deeper connection to my roots, and to my ancestors. Now that I was finally getting to know something about my earliest Wilkins forbearer, I was discovering we had a lot in common.

One thing I did not have in common with John Bird, however, was his elusive nature. The man was full of surprises. How did he manage to transform himself from a farm laborer into an accomplished schoolteacher and then become a Baptist minister?

It does not appear that he received any formal training for his new job. None of the colleges where he claimed to have studied reveal any record of his ever having been a student. However, as the slave of a Presbyterian minister, John Bird would have had plenty of opportunity to become intimately familiar with Christian theology and with the Bible. And it is quite possible that he joined the Baptist church in Oxford as a boy. In the years prior to Emancipation, Oxford's Baptist church welcomed slave members, even those whose masters were not Baptists themselves.[14] The Baptist religion emphasizes the supremacy of personal experience over formal hierarchy; in the early days of the black

Baptist church, the deacons of individual churches had the authority to ordain their own clergy.[15] Perhaps this is how my great-grandfather became a minister. Whatever his formal credentials, John Bird Wilkins possessed two essential qualifications for a life in the ministry: he was a charismatic speaker and a brilliant organizer who knew how to inspire people.

In July 1885 my great-grandfather moved northward with his young bride to begin his new career as the pastor of Pilgrim Baptist Church in St. Paul, Minnesota. Drawn by the prospect of jobs in the city's meatpacking industry, railroads, and hotels, many African Americans migrated to St. Paul after the Civil War. According to local historian Yusef Mgeni, between 1850 and 1890 "a higher percentage of African Americans in Saint Paul owned land and were literate than in any other part of the country."[16]

Located on Sibley Street in the heart of the black community, Pilgrim Baptist Church had been founded in 1866 by Rev. Robert Thomas Hickman and a small band of former slaves from Boone County, Missouri. I do not know how my great-grandfather came to know about this church. It is possible he might have been recommended for his position by a mutual acquaintance in Missouri. John Bird had been the secretary of his lodge back in Memphis, Tennessee, and had organized the construction of a fraternal meeting hall in Farmington. Pastor Hickman was also a Mason, so perhaps the two men had a fraternal connection. When Pastor Hickman retired in 1885, my great-grandfather, now calling himself the Reverend Bird J. Wilkins, became Pilgrim's new pastor.[17]

When I first arrived in Boston, I knew only a handful of people. It took me several years to build a network of friends, and a decade to find a decent job. It seems my great-grandfather was not challenged in either of these departments. Not only did he install himself in a great job despite the lack of any previous experience or formal training, he also went out of his way to be noticed on the local scene. Almost as soon as he arrived in town, he took himself over to the local black paper and introduced himself.[18] And within only a few months of moving to St. Paul, he found himself embroiled in an international controversy.

Louis Riel was the charismatic leader of the mixed-race Métis Indians, a French-speaking tribe whose ancestors included both Europeans and Native Americans. In November 1885, Riel led a bloody revolt against the British authorities in Canada. Riel's trial and ultimate execution by the Canadian government was a subject of heated discussion on both sides of the border. The doomed rebellion would have made a big impact on my great-grandfather. As a former slave with a racially mixed background, he probably took a vicarious satisfaction in seeing another man of mixed race fight so valiantly against white oppression.

In early December 1885, Rev. Bird Wilkins addressed the Riel controversy from his pulpit at Pilgrim Baptist Church. Whatever his formal education may have been, by this point my great-grandfather had become an eloquent speaker whose interests went well beyond conventional religious subjects. The *Christian Recorder,* a black newspaper in Philadelphia, quoted his sermon verbatim under the following headline: "A Defense of Riel. A Sermon by Rev. Bird Wilkins Glorifying Riel as a Patriot Who Will Live in History, and Condemning the Action of Sir John Macdonald."

My great-grandfather's sermon is powerful, articulate, and full of dramatic rhetorical flourishes. "A principle which is a true one can never be blotted out," he states. "The pen of posterity, dipped in the blood of martyrs, will re-write it, or else, with the charcoals of the ruined prosperity of their ancestors, will they mark on memory's pages the hideous sights of a grand and noble principle being burned by the power of an oppressive government."[19]

I was not able to find any record of an official Canadian response to Bird's statements. I did find, however, that his sermon was quoted extensively in a chapter on Riel's rebellion that was written thirty years later by the French Canadian historian Paul Vibert.[20] Clearly, the speech had made enough of an impression in the French-speaking community for Vibert to include it in his history.

Although my great-grandfather remained in St. Paul for less than two years, his pastorate appears to have been a success. Under Bird's leadership the church was able to purchase a lot on Cedar and Summit Streets, where a new, larger church was built.[21] And, in one of his first projects as pastor, my great-grandfather created a literary society where church members met weekly to discuss the literary interests of the day.

In addition to tending to his congregation and raising his young son, Charles, my great-grandfather also published a newspaper while in St. Paul. Published quarterly, the *Pulpit and Desk* was Bird's personal platform. He was its owner, editor, and publisher. Although no copies of the newspaper survive today, Bird would later claim it had a circulation of over five thousand readers.[22]

St. Paul had been good to John Bird Wilkins, providing him a place to hone his new identity as a clergyman. But in the spring of 1887, my great-grandfather decided to uproot his family once again. This time the Wilkins family would be making their new home on the south side of Chicago.

Rev. Bird Wilkins, *Cleveland Gazette,* November 19, 1887

Chapter Eight

The People's Temple, 1887–1888

On April 17, 1887, the *Chicago Daily Inter Ocean* reported, "A New Pastor: The members of Bethesda Baptist Church, Thirty–fourth and Butterfield streets, are jubilant indeed. The cause of it is that they have secured the Rev. Bird Wilkins, B. D. of St. Paul, Minn., for their pastor." According to the article, my great-grandfather was reputed to be "the most eloquent colored preacher in America to-day."[1]

In the 1880s religious leaders were considered celebrity figures by the press. When John Bird gave his first sermon at Bethesda Baptist Church, a *Chicago Tribune* reporter was there to cover the story. Rev. Wilkins is described as "of medium size, slender and graceful build, with very light complexion, and heavy, straight, black hair, which he wears long and combs back from his forehead in a pleasing manner. He has black side whiskers and mustache, but his chin is smooth shaven. In the pulpit he is perfectly self possessed, graceful, and fluent in speech." My great-grandfather's liberal theology impressed the reporter: "Unlike most Baptists, he does not believe in future punishment by fire and brimstone, and says he 'would rather preach no God at all than to preach that my God does all the dire, and dirty, and mean things some preachers say He does.'"[2]

Chicago was the ideal city for a person of Bird Wilkins's broad interests and boundless energy. The city's elite blacks were articulate, college educated, and passionately involved in the issues of the day. The Prudence Crandall Club, founded by journalist Fannie Barrier Williams, held weekly meetings to discuss the latest developments in science, literature, philosophy, and the arts, while Bethel African Methodist Episcopal Church and Quinn Chapel offered lectures by leading intellectuals on Sunday afternoons.[3] These were exciting times, and the Reverend Bird Wilkins, always outspoken, was soon in the thick of a new controversy.

During the summer of 1887, a state law forbidding commerce on Sundays was being debated in the Illinois legislature. On June 13, the Reverend Dr. W. M.

Lawrence, a prominent Chicago clergyman, preached a sermon to his white congregation supporting the bill. Sunday should be a religious—not a civil—holiday, Dr. Lawrence declared. On the same day, on the other side of town, Rev. Bird Wilkins addressed his congregation at Bethesda Baptist Church:

Whenever I think the religion of love given by Jesus needs the arm of the State to support it or protect it I will renounce it. . . . To indorse these Sunday laws as a church is to indorse or to approve one of the festivals of the ancient Sun-god. . . . [H]ow our Protestant divines . . . can defend a law that attempts to consecrate a day which is made holy by the decree of a heathen idolator I do not understand nor can they explain it.

Not only was John Bird opposing the established position of many Protestant ministers, he was also saying that church creeds had no place in civil law. I can only imagine the reaction of his staid congregation to this sermon.[4]

My great-grandfather was not alone in advocating a more secular view of government's role in public affairs. New, more liberal ideas were circulating among the city's intellectuals, and many reformers were calling for change. Chicago in 1887 was a city of economic extremes. While Philip Armour, Marshall Field, and other wealthy businessmen lived in luxurious mansions along the lakefront with retinues of servants at their disposal, Irish, German, and Polish immigrants lived in dilapidated shacks without toilets or running water on the other side of town. It is not surprising that such marked income disparities fostered a state of war between the opposing factions of capital and labor. In May 1886 a bomb exploded during a labor demonstration in Haymarket Square, killing eight policemen. The ensuing trial and subsequent conviction of eight radical labor activists put the whole city on edge.

For most blacks, however, the events surrounding the Haymarket bombing held little interest. In his *Black Chicago's First Century,* historian Christopher Reed points out that "racism on the part of organized labor in the North had excluded African Americans" from participation in the city's industrial sector. "The great conflict between capital and labor playing out on the national stage would not affect blacks in significant numbers until the turn of the next century."[5]

But John Bird Wilkins, always a maverick, paid close attention to the labor issue. Although he had lived in Chicago barely six months, my great-grandfather once again placed himself at the center of a controversy. On August 22, 1887, the *Chicago Tribune* reported, "A Remarkable Sermon: The Rev. Bird Wilkins likens Henry George to Christ." Henry George was a controversial New York politician, editor, and economist who saw unearned wealth as the direct cause of poverty. George also believed that large monopolies such as railroads and power companies should be nationalized, and that land—rather than income—should be taxed. John Bird must have known that the very mention of George's name would cause a stir among Chicago's wealthy citizens.

The *Tribune,* after describing Rev. Wilkins as "a man of fine personal appearance" who was "gifted with a fluent tongue," quotes extensively from my great-grandfather's sermon. Telling his congregation that Jesus "preached and practiced Communism," John Bird reminded his listeners of the parable of the vineyard, in which the workers who were hired late in the day and only worked one hour "received as much pay as those who had worked eleven hours through the heat of the day. Why? Because their needs were as great as those who had worked eleven hours." John Bird Wilkins was, after all, a former slave and a man intimately acquainted with poverty. In this sermon he criticized the government's failure to better the lives of the nation's poor: "We have no business to have poverty in the United States. To say that our Government is all right is foolishness. . . . The world is not fit to live in now. Christians living on the first, second and third floors of a house and a Christian committing suicide from want and starvation on the fourth floor." My great-grandfather concluded his sermon with a challenge to his congregation: "Brother Jones has $600; Sister Smith has $2,000 in the bank; Brother Johnson has a house and a lot. They give their worldly possessions to the church and we all share alike. Do you know what would happen? The spirit of God would descend upon the people, men would speak with tongues of fire, the millennium would reign, and Heaven would be upon the earth."[6]

I love this sermon. It is, as the newspaper headline promised, quite remarkable. However, in 1887, Bethesda Baptist was still a relatively new church, competing with more established churches for worshippers to fill its brand-new sanctuary. The radical theology of their unconventional new pastor was not likely to bring Bethesda many new converts. For most African American churchgoers, life was a daily struggle just to put food on the table. When they went to church on Sunday, these hardworking folks sought reassurance, not controversy.[7]

John Bird was unrepentant, however. In an acerbic letter to the *Tribune's* editor the following week, he defended his sermon and fired off a broadside against the "green-eyed monopolists, the soulless corporations which devour all the honey" that plain working people bring into society. The rich enjoy the sweets, while working people can "scarcely keep body and soul together."[8] In an era when blacks were virtually invisible in the white press, my great-grandfather's unconventional take on the standard pieties and his witty, irreverent delivery made him a good source of news. He was even quoted in the *New Orleans Daily Picayune:* "Rev. Bird Wilkins of Chicago says good bread, tender steak, nicely cooked potatoes and clear, fragrant coffee at breakfast will do more to make a man a Christian than soggy bread, burnt toast and warmed over coffee, followed by an hour and a half of Bible reading and family prayers."[9]

A more conservative person might have thought it prudent to assume a lower profile. John Bird was, after all, a relatively new minister, with a large and conservative congregation to represent. But, it seems, prudence was not one of my great-grandfather's main attributes. Within the month he would involve himself in an even more controversial situation. In 1887 Rev. Lloyd Jenkins opened the doors of his previously all-white Unitarian Church to Chicago's African Americans. Although only a few black intellectuals worshipped at All Souls church regularly, my great-grandfather took notice.[10]

The Unitarian denomination encourages discussion and intellectual enquiry; it does not require its members to adhere to any particular creed or dogma. Unlike the Baptists and most other Christians, Unitarians do not believe in the divinity of Jesus. Rather, they accept religious pluralism and find value in the teachings of many different spiritual traditions. Unitarians believe that Christ's table should be open to all comers. Baptists, on the other hand, believe that only people who are of the Baptist faith should receive communion. At Bethesda Baptist Church, John Bird began to offer an "open" communion, allowing Christians of different denominations to participate in the sacrament.[11] As my great-grandfather moved further from the philosophical underpinnings of the Baptist faith, his congregation became increasingly uncomfortable and irritated.

Even before he gave his sermon in praise of Henry George, John Bird had begun receiving threats from irate members of his congregation. On July 1, 1887, he received this anonymous letter:

MR. WILKINS: It affords us with pleasure to let you know if the Baptists dont put a stop to your having open communion we will put a stop if you do it again. You cant live in Chicago if we cant get you one way we will get you another. We thought you were a gentleman or we would not try to support you but as it is, the sooner you get out of Chicago the better for you. We will see whether you come here and put down the Baptist cause to suit yourself. If you want to commune with the Methodist you better live with them no more insults we want to here.[12]

Things at Bethesda had clearly reached a crisis point. My great-grandfather, it seems, would have to step back from his unorthodox practices or leave the church. On September 5, 1887, John Bird Wilkins addressed a letter to his congregation: "Deacons, Officers, and Members of Bethesda Church,—Dear friends: Being no longer in sympathy with the Baptist denomination, I hereby tender you my resignation as pastor, which I hope will take effect in accordance with our agreement. This resignation will not be recalled. It must be accepted."[13]

That same week, John Bird sat down with a reporter from the *Chicago Tribune*. In this interview, my great-grandfather spoke about the reasons for his resignation:

I believe in the fatherly kindness of God. The old idea of a God of vengeance, ready to burn up the world in hell-fire, is opposed to reason and common sense and abhorrent to me. I no longer endorse the doctrine of the Trinity, nor can I swallow the three persons in one and all omnipotent. My belief is that the Bible has a divine and human line of thought running through it; there is much good in the Bible and a great deal that is the entire opposite. I preached a sermon which caused a great fuss in my congregation, in which I showed that slavery, polygamy, Communism, murder, intemperance, and Socialism were not only taught by precept in the bible, but also by example. I am also a free believer in open communion: that a Methodist, Presbyterian, Catholic, or a member of any denomination is entitled to the sacrament at my hands as well as a Baptist. I have acted on this belief, and this has been a constant cause of dissatisfaction to a minority of my flock.[14]

Millions of today's Christians continue to believe that every word of the Bible is divinely inspired, and the Trinitarian Divinity of Father, Son, and Holy Spirit remains the cornerstone of standard Christian theology. My great-grandfather's views would be considered provocative in many contemporary churches. In 1887 they would have been utterly shocking.

When asked about his future plans, John Bird told the *Tribune*'s reporter: "I am going to stay in Chicago and build a large church, to be known as 'Liberty Temple.' I have already collected subscriptions amounting to $9,200, and any necessary amount can be obtained from my sympathizers. Here the liberal minded colored people of all denominations will be gathered, and I intend to show Chicago and the world a new sight—an advancing and progressing colored congregation."[15]

On October 9, 1887, the first service of John Bird's new church was held at the Freiberg Opera House. Once again, my great-grandfather's activities earned him media attention. Philadelphia's *Christian Recorder* reported that he had been offered a hundred dollars a night (a hefty sum of money for the time) to lecture for the Rockport Lecture Association. The *Milwaukee Sentinel* commented that John Bird's new church would be "the first African Unitarian Church in the history of the world." Boston's *Congregationalist* took a dimmer view: "If we are to judge this movement by other similar ones that were to turn the world upside down, it will hardly be heard of again."[16]

I do not know how my great-grandmother felt about the controversy swirling around her husband. Just a few weeks earlier, Susie had given birth to Byrd, the couple's second son. Now that John Bird had resigned his steady position at Bethesda, the family had no reliable source of income and two small children to feed. My great-grandmother was a small-town girl who was still only nineteen in 1887. Like most women of her day, she had probably been raised to regard her husband as the unequivocal king of the family. Although John Bird's flamboyant activities may have caused concern, I doubt whether Susie questioned them.

In November 1887, my great-grandfather met with a reporter from the *Cleveland Gazette*. In this interview, John Bird, exuding confidence and optimism, states that he has just been offered an editing position at the *Chicago Illustrated Graphic News,* "the largest and probably the best illustrated weekly paper published west of New York." The *Gazette,* an African American newspaper, made much of the fact that my great-grandfather would now be working for a white weekly. The article goes on to mention John Bird's growing national prominence: "He is pronounced by many as the leading colored minister in the city, if not in the country, as well as the leading colored journalist."[17]

As 1887 drew to a close, John Bird Wilkins seems to have been on the verge of an exciting new life. Fund-raising for his new church was proceeding apace, a new job was in the offing, and the national media was taking notice. But so, apparently, were some disgruntled Baptists.

On January 6, 1888, the *Chicago Tribune* printed the following story: "Wilkins Is Persecuted: The Pastor of Liberty Church in Hard Lines. The residence of the Rev. Bird J. Wilkins was partially burned last Sunday night, and thereby hangs a tale. Bird J. Wilkins was formerly pastor of the Bethesda Baptist Church, and preached to the largest colored congregation in the city." After describing John Bird as "a young man of pleasing personal appearance and of more than average intelligence," the paper reports that, while he was preaching at a Sunday night service nearby, John Bird's home was intentionally set ablaze. According to the *Tribune,* John Bird received this letter the day after the fire:

CITY, Jan. 5, 1888, Mr. Wilkins—We have warned you that you cannot preach against orthodox religion. We believe you are tending a religion from the devil and we set your house afire in three places but it burned in only one. We will kill you before you shall hurt us with your new religion. Our white orthodox churches tell us to run you out of this town and you have got to go. If you stay you will do so at the risk of your life. we tell you in time. This is our last warning. We don't want to hurt you, but you must leave this place. Now get out as quick as you can. AN ORTHODOX"

The article goes on to describe my great-grandfather's response to the threats. "I have no clew as to who wrote the letter, but would give considerable to find out," he is reported as saying. "I could not give much money, the fire having destroyed everything I have except a few books. The fire also burned all the threatening letters but the one of July 1, which as you see, is scorched and partly burned. All the letters were in different hand-writing, most of them plainly in a disguised hand." When asked by the *Tribune*'s reporter if he had been threatened personally, my great-grandfather replied: "Yes, several times. Just before I resigned in the early part of September, Louis Wills of No. 1643 State street, came up to me in church one Sunday night, put his hand to his hip-pocket, and threatened to shoot me. The women were worse than the men. Mrs. Tim Cooper, No. 4509 Dearborn street, threatened to cowhide me on sight. I have not met her since."

John Bird's Unitarian views had riled other ministers in the black community as well as the members of his own congregation. He told the *Tribune:*

All the orthodox preachers have warned their congregations against me and said I was in league with the devil. . . . With them a person [who] is not an orthodox Baptist is about the same as a Socialist or an Anarchist. They take exception to my doctrine that there is not a personal devil and no literal hell. I have known all along that there were persons very bitter against me, but have thought that a man too cowardly to sign his name would be too cowardly to burn a house. The rapid growth of my church has probably made them desperate.

When asked whether he intended to leave town, my great-grandfather replied passionately: "Never in the world. I have been threatened by the Ku-Klux of South Carolina when I taught school there after the war. They burned my school and I taught the poor colored children out doors under the trees. I am not scared by a lot of cowards whose only weapon is the incendiary's torch. I have called the attention of the city authorities and the Fire Department to the case and expect to discover the guilty parties."[18]

I have always been a bit of a maverick. When all my friends were teasing their hair and dreaming about the senior prom, I was hanging out in jazz clubs learning how to play the drums. I am leery of traveling in lockstep with any kind of group mentality, particularly where matters of the spirit are concerned, and it pains me to imagine John Bird being persecuted for his unconventional beliefs. Although my great-grandfather appears defiant in his newspaper interview, the burning of his home must have shaken him. Even if he were unafraid for his own safety, he would have had his young wife and two small children to think about.

I do not know how long John Bird stayed in Chicago after the arson attack. The position he had hoped for with the *Illustrated Graphic News* never materialized. It is possible that my great-grandfather met the paper's editor—Benjamin Franklin Underwood, a prominent Unitarian journalist and freethinker—through a mutual connection in the Unitarian Church. But in the few copies of the *Illustrated Graphic News* that survive, John Bird Wilkins's name is not listed among the paper's employees.

Without a steady job to support him, it was only a matter of time before my great-grandfather would be driven out of town. After 1888 his name no longer appears in the Chicago city directory. Although he would live another fifty-three years, I could not find any evidence that the Reverend Bird J. Wilkins ever led another church.

J. B. WILKINS.
AGRICULTURAL MACHINE.

No. 484,690.   Patented Oct. 18, 1892.

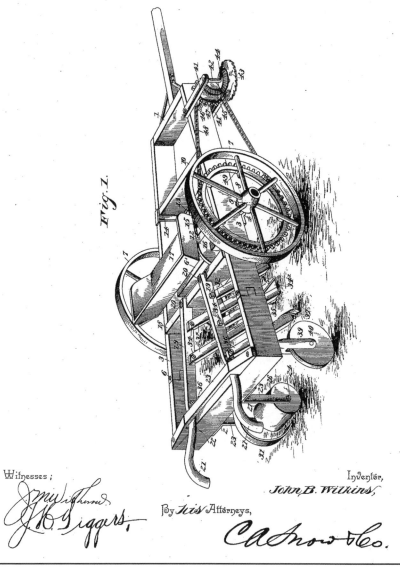

Fig. 1.

Witnesses;

Inventor,
John B. Wilkins,

By *his* Attorneys,

Agricultural machine designed by John Bird Wilkins

Chapter Nine

The Bigamist, 1889–1915

After my great-grandfather left Chicago, he seems to have moved his family back to Farmington, Missouri. There, Susie gave birth to their third child, Aravelle, in 1889. In January 1891 Mary Corinne, their fourth child and only girl, was born.

I do not know exactly how my great-grandfather supported his family during this period. Farmington was a small rural community, and there would have been little work in town for an intellectual maverick such as John Bird Wilkins. Perhaps he taught school, though no record survives of his having done so. My great-grandfather had been a farm hand in Mississippi. He seems to have returned to agricultural work in order to support his family while in Farmington. At that time many African American men in the area supported themselves this way.[1]

Although he may have been working as a farm laborer, he continued to find outlets for his restless intellect, however. On April 16, 1892, he submitted drawings to the U.S. Patent Office for a new invention. He called it simply his "Agricultural Machine" and claimed his invention would combine the functions of several different machines: "My invention relates to agricultural machines: and the objects in view are to provide a machine adapted to serve as a cotton planter, scraper, and cultivator or chopper, and as a road-cart, and also adapted as a cotton and cornstalk cutter."[2]

The drawings of the device are elaborate and beautiful. By making a few easy changes in the gears, my great-grandfather's machine could sow the seed, till the crop, harvest it, and then serve as a cart to carry it to market. But despite its ingenuity, the Agricultural Machine seems not to have been widely used. I could not find any evidence that its patent was ever renewed, and it is not mentioned in contemporary news accounts.

My great-grandfather had tasted the action, intellectual stimulation, and ferment of life in Chicago. By 1893 he must have found Farmington stultifying. Disgraced as a minister, John Bird had been forced to return to farm life in the provincial town he had left six years earlier with such high hopes. On top of everything else, he now had a wife and four small mouths to feed.

It is easy to imagine relations between John Bird and Susie growing strained during this period. I doubt if my great-grandmother in her worst nightmares could have envisioned her current circumstances. Nor can I imagine that her parents, founding members of the St. Paul Methodist Church, would have approved of John Bird's maverick beliefs or flamboyant behavior.

There was also the matter of Lena Murphy.

The historical record of Lena's relationship with my great-grandfather is murky, to say the least. There are no marriage licenses, birth certificates, or census records available with which to track the couple's movements before 1893. This research obstacle is further compounded by the fact that, when giving their names to census takers in Missouri and Arkansas, they both appear to have deliberately given false information. It took my researcher, Mariah Cooper, months to uncover John Bird and Lena Murphy's tracks and more months of reading between the lines in old newspaper articles and the birth records of their children to confirm her findings.

My best guess is that John Bird Wilkins and Lena Murphy first became involved somewhere between 1892 and the beginning of 1893. He would have been roughly forty years of age, while Lena would have just turned seventeen. Along with Susie Douthit's family, Lena Murphy's parents attended St. Paul Methodist Church.[3] It is likely that the two women knew each other well. Although Lena was five or six years younger than Susie, the two women may even have been friends, which would have made John Bird's infidelity all the more difficult for my great-grandmother to bear.

In early 1893 John Bird moved to Little Rock, Arkansas, and set up a home at 18th and Ringo Streets.[4] Lena most likely moved with him, and she gave birth to John Bird's son there on December 15, 1893. In a tribute to his ambitions as a public speaker and theologian, John Bird named his child Edward Everett Horton Wilkins after the famous Unitarian clergyman.

Whether Susie knew that John Bird and Lena Murphy were living together at this point is uncertain. Perhaps my great-grandmother assumed that her husband was simply away from Farmington on business. After all, John Bird had family in Oxford, and the business partner for his Agricultural Machine lived in Vicksburg. Even if she suspected that he was cheating on her, I doubt my great-grandmother knew that John Bird had already begun a new family with Lena Murphy in Little Rock.

Susie must have hoped against hope that she could win her husband back. In the early summer of 1893, she and John Bird conceived another child. When my grandfather, Jesse Ernest Wilkins, was born on February 1, 1894, perhaps Susie believed that the baby's presence would reinvigorate her marriage.

But Susie's relationship with John Bird was finished. By 1894 my great-grandfather was living in Little Rock, most likely with Lena and their son, Edward. His new family seems to have moved frequently. There is no record that they remained in any one place for more than a year between 1892 and 1900, but the birthplaces of their children give us some idea of where the couple lived during this time. The oldest, Edward Everett Wilkins, was born in Little Rock in 1893. The next, Howard, was born in Oxford, Mississippi, in 1894, the same year my grandfather was born in Farmington. Sometime around 1896 the couple moved to Drew County, Arkansas, where two more children, Henry and John Brooksy, were born.[5]

The federal census shows my great-grandfather and his new family living in Drew County in 1900. John Bird is now calling himself Howard R. Wilkins. He and Lena Murphy (who tells the census man her name is Susie) are working as laborers on a rented farm in Bartholomew Township.[6] Exactly why John Bird chose to call himself Howard is unclear. But the fact that Lena also doesn't use her correct name leads me to speculate that the couple did not want too much official attention focused on them. Perhaps John Bird thought that, if his new location became public, the Baptists who set fire to his Chicago home or some of Susie Douthit's angry relatives might come looking for him. It is easy to imagine that my great-grandfather could have embroiled himself in an entirely new controversy that might have given him and Lena additional reasons to disguise their identities—reasons that, for now at least, have been lost to history.

Back in Farmington, Susie struggled to make a life for herself. I'm guessing the black folks in town knew all about John Bird's affair and his illicit family. The town was just too small for a scandal like that to remain hidden. Even if no one said anything out loud, there would have been skeptical glances when Susie went shopping on Main Street and plenty of juicy gossip to pass around with the fried chicken after church on Sundays. But Susan Olivia Douthit was a survivor. Although John Bird's desertion must have been both financially devastating and emotionally painful, my great-grandmother had five small children to feed. By the summer of 1900, Susie had found a job working as a domestic servant.[7]

I was brought up in the age of the dishwasher, the microwave, and the electric can opener, so it is hard for me to picture what my great-grandmother's daily life might have been like. In his book *Seven Days a Week*, David Katzman offers a detailed description of the typical week's work for a domestic servant during this period: "Daily chores for the maid of all work included lighting fires (in stoves, for hot water, in winter fireplaces or furnaces), preparing and serving meals and cleaning up, making beds, doing light dusting, sweeping or scrubbing front steps and porch, answering the doorbell, and running errands." In addition to this daily work, Susie would have been expected to wash, iron, and mend clothes; wash and polish the dishes and the silver; wash the windows; clean out the cellar; and on Saturdays, bake bread. "Repetition of tasks made the work monotonous, but the complaint heard most seemed to be that of physical fatigue and tiredness," Katzman states. "Over and over again women mentioned how they often collapsed in bed at the end of the day, too tired to read or even take a bath."[8]

The thought of doing that much manual labor every day while taking care of five small children boggles my mind. When I first moved to Boston twenty-five years ago, I was a single mother for three years. And believe me, there were plenty of nights when, between my full-time job teaching music at a local high school, my part-time job playing gigs with an aspiring blues band, and the all-the-time job of raising my five-year-old daughter, I thought I would lose my mind.

My great-grandmother must have been one tough cookie. I know that if I had been Susie, there would have been no crying, whining, or complaining allowed when I came home from work in the evening. Although my grandfather was the pampered baby of the family, he would have been expected to shoulder his own burdens at an early age. Sitting around feeling sorry for oneself was a luxury the child of a black domestic at the turn of the century was not likely to enjoy.

John Bird, meanwhile, had moved his other family out of Little Rock again, this time to the tiny lumber town of Crossett in Ashley County, Arkansas. By 1910 my great-grandfather, now calling himself Hayward B. Wilkins, was working at the local sawmill. In this census he lives in a rented house with Lena (who is still calling herself Susie). The couple now has nine children, ranging in age from six months to sixteen years.[9]

During this period of his life, John Bird seems to have been occupied completely with supporting his second family. Although Crossett's black community boasted a Baptist church and its own newspaper, I was not able to find any evidence of his preaching, inventing, or writing anything between 1893 and 1915. Nor has history left us any clue as to how he occupied his restless intellect during these years. Perhaps he kept in touch with some of his Masonic brothers from the old days. Surely he kept up with the news and followed world events in whatever local papers were available. It must have hurt a man so brilliant and so enamored of the spotlight to have to live the life of an anonymous laborer, but this is exactly what my great-grandfather seems to have done: work hard, support his new family, and lay low.

Back in Farmington, Susie soon adjusted to the new rhythms of her single life. By the summer of 1910 she owned her own home on Cayce Street in the center of town. Her three eldest children, Charles, Byrd, and Aravelle, had all moved out and were making successful lives for themselves. The fourth child, Corinne, still lived at home but had a job working as a cook for a white family. Even my grandfather, J. Ernest, had found work as a laborer even though he was only sixteen.[10]

At this time, Susie was making her living as a laundress. Although it was physically demanding, many black women actually preferred laundry work to domestic service. A washerwoman could negotiate her own price, set her own hours, and work in her own home at her own pace.[11] At that time a woman in Farmington could earn between fifty and seventy-five cents for every load of laundry she did.[12] When I read this, I didn't think fifty cents was any money at all, but then I realized that in 1910 it was possible to buy an entire meal at a restaurant for a nickel.

In exchange for the cash she earned, a laundry woman put in hours of back-breaking labor. The gallons of water used for washing, boiling, and rinsing clothes had to be carried bucket by bucket from the pump and poured into large wooden washtubs. In addition to washing the clothes, washerwomen often made their own soap from lye and their own starch from wheat bran. Some washerwomen even made their own washtubs by cutting beer barrels in half. After getting the water, tubs, and soap ready, Susie would have had to sort the clothes into four separate categories—whites, coarse whites, flannels, and colored clothes. Each fabric type required its own water temperature and had to be scrubbed and soaked in its own separate tub.[13]

Then she would put the wet clothes through the ringer and hang them out to dry. If the weather was nice, she would have hung them in the yard outside. In bad weather, there would have been wet clothes strung across the main room of the house, occupying every spare bit of space.[14]

After the clothes dried, they had to be ironed. The irons used at that time were heavy as they were made of iron. Each iron was heated on the stove, and then, after she had sprayed the clothes with starch, she would have lifted this weight countless times in order to press the clothes into shape. It's little wonder that laundry work was considered one of the most physically demanding domestic chores of the era.[15]

By 1910, it seems, my great-grandmother had given up on John Bird and was moving on with her life. I noted with a wry smile that in the 1910 census, she gives her marital status as "widow."[16] Maybe she knew her husband was still living. But clearly, she no longer cared. He was dead as far as she was concerned.

In fact, John Bird Wilkins would continue living for another twenty-eight years, and somewhere around 1915, he and his other family moved to St. Louis. According to a brief clipping Mariah Cooper found, in 1915 John Bird (now calling himself Dr. H. B. Wilkins) was invited to participate in a "Committee of 100" of St. Louis's community leaders, to "help with the war effort." In this brief article, my great-grandfather is referred to as the "editor" of the *St. Louis Clarion*.[17] But as was often the case with John Bird Wilkins, I was having a hard time finding evidence of his participation on the *Clarion*.

No copies of the paper survived, at least not in the libraries around Boston. When I mentioned my frustrations to Mariah Cooper, she suggested that I plan a research trip to the St. Louis area. Perhaps I would find copies of the *Clarion* there. Copies of the *St. Louis Argus*, the region's major African American newspaper, were on microfilm at the St. Louis County Library; perhaps there might be articles in the *Argus* about either John Bird Wilkins or J. Ernest? While I was in the area, Mariah suggested, I could drive out to Farmington and see whether there were any records about my grandfather or his mother, Susie Douthit, in the local archives. Perhaps I might even be able to track a bit more of John Bird's early career as a teacher there?

But I was getting tired. After nearly two years of research, I had discovered information that had been lost to my family for two generations. With Mariah's expert help I had tracked John Bird Wilkins and Lena Murphy throughout Missouri, Arkansas, and Mississippi. I had uncovered a variety of aliases and had managed to account for much of their lives between 1894 and 1910, but each answer I found seemed just to generate even more questions.

What eventually happened to my great-grandfather? Did he know that his son J. Ernest went on to become a successful attorney? Did J. Ernest ever reconnect with his father? Had his father's presence (or absence) had any effect on my grandfather's character? And finally, what—if anything—did any of this information have to do with J. Ernest's abrupt departure from the Department of Labor in 1958?

Truth was, I was beginning to feel a bit like Don Quixote. I felt as if I was tilting at windmills. Maybe it was time to give my research obsession a rest? I returned to the rest of my life. I taught my students and played the piano, but each time I meditated at my ancestors' altar, something nagged at me. Had I really done everything I could to honor Aunt Marjory's memory and to preserve the history of the Wilkins family?

A few weeks later I got a letter from Mariah Cooper. She had not been able to find anything new about my great-grandfather's life between 1910 and 1915, but she had uncovered a woman named Ethel Porter, a distant relative on Aunt Marjory's side of the family. Mrs. Porter was the granddaughter of a slave named Jeremiah McFarland, and she was about to celebrate her one-hundredth birthday.

I was flabbergasted. All the Wilkins children had grown up hearing Aunt Marjory tell us that our family's first ancestor was an African named Jeremiah.

According to Aunt Marj, he had been brought to this country from Madagascar and sold into slavery on the docks of New York in the late 1700s. At this point in the recitation, Aunt Marj would shake her head dramatically and announce: "Jeremiah was a *slave*. He was from *Africa!*" I had long ago given up hope of finding any tangible connection to this mythological figure. Since Aunt Marj's story about J. Ernest's father had turned out to be a complete fiction, I doubted her Jeremiah story would be any more reliable.

At the same time, however, I was curious. Who knows? Perhaps Aunt Marjory really did have a slave ancestor named Jeremiah. I got Ethel Porter's address and sent a birthday card telling her who I was and how I thought we might be related. As an afterthought I also sent Mrs. Porter a dozen roses. It's not often a person lives to celebrate their one-hundredth birthday, and the least I could do was to show my respect to a family elder.

A few weeks later, an envelope arrived in the mail, containing a handwritten note and a few typewritten sheets of paper: "Ms. Wilkins—Hope this finds you well. Here is a rough draft of my family History. My grandmother, Ethel Porter, has been wanting me to organize this and send it to you. I also have many old family pictures to go along with this story. All the best, 'Chris.'"[18]

With trembling hands I unfolded the typewritten sheets and began to read:

Porter Family History—Jeffersonville, IN
Our family history begins with an Irish immigrant who met a Native American woman; they bore a daughter named Zoe who would become a slave. In those days, kids could be hired to work if a family owed money. She was originally supposed to work and in return for labor pay off family debts. These debts would never be paid and Zoe was sold into slavery. Zoe had two daughters, Caroline and Sarah. . . . Sarah married a field slave named Jeremiah MacFarland.[19]

There he was. The mythical Jeremiah! Maybe I hadn't been able to trace him all the way back to Africa, but at least he existed. My excitement mounted as I read on: "It was said that Jerry heard a voice one day while working in the fields. This voice instructed Jerry to go and read the Bible, as an illiterate slave this was a miracle. Jerry read and learned the Bible while working in the fields, he became so well versed in this that he eventually became a preacher."

In addition, Jeremiah was also a skilled carpenter. His master was so pleased with his craftsmanship that Jerry was allowed to keep some of the profits from the furniture he made. But when Mr. McFarland went bankrupt, Jerry, Sarah, and their children were all put up for sale.

Chris's narrative continued: "It is said that at the sale Sarah was holding her baby tightly in hopes that they would not be separated. Unfortunately her attempt failed and Sarah was sold apart from her child. Due to her Sadness, Sarah raised such a calamity that the people who purchased Sarah felt sorry for her and enabled the baby and mother to remain together."

Through all of this, Jeremiah continued to make and sell furniture, saving his profits until he was able to purchase his freedom, and a few years later, that of his daughter Carrie. Promising to return for his wife, Jeremiah took his daughter to live across the Ohio River in the free state of Indiana. According to Chris's narrative, Jeremiah ultimately returned to Louisville and smuggled Sarah to freedom with the help of the Underground Railroad.

I was getting goose bumps. Before opening the mail, I had put a teapot on to boil. Now the kettle had been shrieking for the last several minutes, but I couldn't stop reading long enough to turn off the flame. "Carrie eventually had a daughter and named her Juanita, they resided in Evansville, Indiana. Juanita married Reverend John Robinson from Jeffersonville, Indiana. . . . Juanita and Reverend Robinson had two daughters, Lucile and Marjorie. Lucile later married a man named J. Ernest Wilkins, an attorney in Chicago."

At last my research was turning full circle. I had found a connection to Jeremiah, and one between Jeremiah and my grandfather. In a daze I turned off the flame under my teapot, fixed myself a cup of tea, and read Chris's letter all over again, savoring each sentence. In his letter Chris also mentioned that he had pictures to go along with his narrative. He didn't say who was in the pictures, but it occurred to me that Chris might even have a picture of Jeremiah. "Amazing! Absolutely amazing!" I mumbled to myself as I read.

It was only on my third time through the letter that I really looked at the return address. Chris Wright lived right outside of St. Louis. I had to laugh. Just as I am about to abandon my search, new evidence appears out of the blue, which takes me to where I was thinking of going anyway. Thank you, Aunt Marjory, I thought to myself. So I guess I go to St. Louis after all.

"We are fa-mi-ly," I sang, gaily pounding the kitchen table.

As soon as school was out for the summer, my husband and I contacted Chris and made arrangements to spend a week in St. Louis.

J. Ernest and Lucile

Chapter Ten

St. Louis

"Look! There's the Arch!" I poked my husband in the ribs and pointed. From our vantage point in the sky, the Mississippi River looked like a giant dragon coiling its way through the lush Missouri flatland. The moment our flight landed, I was up and out of my seat, eager to get started on the next phase of the research. Consulting the map I had purchased in anticipation of our adventures, I discovered that Washington Park Cemetery, the final resting place of John Bird Wilkins, was literally ten minutes from the airport.

Perfect, I thought to myself. First things first. Time to say hello to my ancestors.

Washington Park Cemetery is located on the edge of the city, bordered on one side by a major highway and on the other side by Lambert Airport. In 1938 when my great-grandfather was buried, St. Louisans spent their eternal lives in worlds rigidly segregated by race. White people buried their dead in nearby Oak Grove or Valhalla Cemeteries, while members of St. Louis's striving black middle class were laid to rest in Washington Park Cemetery. Christopher K. Robinson, John Bird's boss at the *St. Louis Clarion,* had been interred here, along with two of my grandfather's older brothers, Aravelle and Charles.

Turning off a busy road dotted by fast-food chains and cheap hotels, John edged our rental car through the sagging wrought-iron gates that guarded the entrance to the graveyard. Despite jet planes roaring overhead and six lanes of cars whooshing past on the expressway, the place gave off an air of profound solitude. A placard near the entranceway proclaimed that Washington Park Cemetery was a historic landmark and gave an address where donations could be sent. Judging from the condition of the grounds, fund-raising efforts had not gone well. The place was deserted. The small frame building that had once served as the cemetery's office sat empty, its windows covered by boards. The grass had not been mowed recently, and many tombstones had toppled over.

Although my researcher, Mariah Cooper, had provided me with the plot number, I now realized that finding my great-grandfather's grave was not going to be easy. John took the western half of the graveyard, and I took the eastern half, but our work was hampered by the fact that large sections of the cemetery had been allowed to return to the wild. Methodically, we picked our way through the brambles, stumbling over the uneven ground as we searched for a marker or plot number that would enable us to find John Bird's grave. It had rained recently; the grass was heavy and wet. Tombstones leaned crazily amid the trees, hanging vines, thickets of bramble, dense underbrush, and dead animals.

Scraping my shin against a half-submerged headstone, I recalled Mariah Cooper telling me that my great-grandfather might not even be buried here anymore. When the airport was expanded several years ago, a number of Washington Park's bodies had been moved to other cemeteries around the city. Weird depressions in the sodden earth marked spots where graves had been removed, or perhaps just flooded out. As I stepped over a large tangle of vines swallowing up yet another tombstone, I prayed that John Bird's body would still be here and that his grave, unlike many of the others I passed, would have a proper stone to mark its place.

When I finally spotted his headstone, I couldn't stop myself from shouting. The Wilkins family had either had extremely good foresight or perhaps were just plain lucky. They buried my great-grandfather on the high ground.

"I've found him! I've found him!" I hollered, running heedlessly through the wet grass. "John Bird's grave is still here." Inscribed simply with the word "Wilkins," a granite tombstone marked the spot where my great-grandfather was buried, together with Lena Murphy and four of their children. I laid a bouquet of flowers on the ground next to his tombstone, and I knelt down to have a chat.

"Well, John Bird. I am here to greet you at last. I bring you greetings and salutations from your 'other' family, and hope that you are having a peaceful afterlife. Whether you made it to Heaven or not, I don't know. I guess only God can judge. But now I need your help. Please help me reclaim the history of the Wilkins family and find out what really happened to J. Ernest in Washington."

As I was speaking, my eyes filled with tears. They couldn't have been tears of mourning. After all, John Bird had been dead for many years by the time I was born. I was profoundly happy to find my great-grandfather after a search of more than two years, so maybe I was shedding tears of joy. Or perhaps my tears simply reflected my frustration with human mortality in general. Did we really think we could stave off our ultimate extinction by building these pitiful stone markers to tell ensuing generations that we had, in fact, been here? What did it all matter, anyway? Washington Park Cemetery offered all the proof anyone needed to understand that our physical presence here on earth is fragile and short-lived. The old saying in the Bible had it right: ashes to ashes, dust to dust.

As John and I drove out of Washington Park's sagging wrought-iron gates and back into the twenty-first century, I made myself a promise. I would not rest until I had done everything I could to document and preserve my family's history for future generations. Time may be impossible to defeat, but through the telling of the family story, it can at least be extended. After checking into our motel near the airport, John and I drove to the St. Louis County Library on Lindbergh Road. Here, we hoped to find copies of the *St. Louis Clarion,* where John Bird worked. We would also look for any articles about him in the *St. Louis Argus.* Stepping inside the library, I was quickly disabused of the notion that I was the only person on the planet interested in finding out about my ancestors. The St. Louis County Library has an entire floor devoted to genealogical research, and every table was filled with researchers digging through old directories or scrolling through microfilm. John and I made ourselves comfortable, collected several rolls of microfilm from the librarian, and for the next several hours lost ourselves in reading about the black history of St. Louis.

In 1860 a farmer named Charles M. Elleard purchased a tract of land just outside St. Louis. On this land Elleard raised horses, grew crops, and operated a horticulture center. This area eventually became the town Elleardsville, known to local residents as "The Ville." After the town was annexed by the City of St. Louis in 1876, African Americans began to settle there in increasing numbers. Soon The Ville was home to two large black churches—Antioch Baptist, organized in 1878, and St. James African Methodist Episcopal, organized in 1881. The African American population in St. Louis grew by 60 percent between 1910 and 1920. As blacks from the South flooded into the city seeking greater employment opportunities, The Ville became the undisputed center of black St. Louis. Sumner High School, the first secondary school for African Americans west of the Mississippi, was built in The Ville in 1910, followed by John Marshall Elementary School in 1918.[1]

In 1917 the African American hair products tycoon Annie Malone built an office building in The Ville at the corner of St. Ferdinand and Pendleton Avenues. Occupying an entire city block, the building housed the company's office, its manufacturing plant, and Poro College, where hundreds of beauticians were trained to dispense Malone's products throughout the country. Poro College became a central gathering place and symbol of pride for the neighborhood, and it hosted concerts, lectures, and community activities.[2]

In an era without television or radio, people depended on the college's programs to keep them abreast of the latest developments. A well-informed person might read as many as three newspapers a day. Since the white media rarely covered events taking place in the black community, African Americans created their own newspapers. By 1920 there were fifty-four black-owned newspapers in the state of Missouri alone. As the epicenter of black St. Louis, The Ville was home to three black newspapers during this period.[3]

In 1912 J. E. and William Mitchell began to publish the *St. Louis Argus* as a weekly community newspaper. Supported by the city's Republican Party machine, the *Argus* could be purchased at groceries, newsstands, and shoe-shine parlors throughout the black community. The *Argus* documented the doings of St. Louis's growing black population. It also gave its readers an African American editorial perspective on national and international events.[4] When the St. Louis city council passed a segregation ordinance in 1916 that barred blacks from owning or renting property in white neighborhoods, the *Argus* waged an editorial war to get the legislation defeated. When the U.S. Supreme Court declared the ordinance unconstitutional, the paper celebrated with banner-sized headlines.

At the end of the First World War, the *Argus* had become successful enough to purchase new office space on Market Street. The building was valued at over thirty thousand dollars and contained offices, a meeting hall, and a ballroom.[5] By this time the *Argus* was the major source of news not only for African Americans in St. Louis but for blacks throughout the state. The *Argus* reported on the doings of Farmington's black folk in a special column written by Dayse Baker.

Sitting in the St. Louis County Library more than eighty years later, John and I read about the school graduations, church socials, and parties that formed the fabric of Farmington's black social life in the years after the First World War. "Mr. Arvilla Wilkins and wife are enjoying a pleasant week with their mother, Mrs. S. O. Wilkins. Farmington delights in the intellectual activity of its young people. Miss Corinne Wilkins will soon assume the work of teaching in the Coffman vicinity," Baker noted in her column on November 21, 1915. When Corinne, J. Ernest's older sister, came back to visit her mother the following month, Baker reported it. When my grandfather returned home from college for Christmas that year, Baker reported it, referring to him as "Ernestine," the name by which he had been known in elementary school.[6] My grandfather changed his name to J. Ernest during his first year at Lincoln, but to his elders in Farmington he was still Ernestine, Susie Wilkins's youngest boy.

The *Argus* was unabashedly Republican and made no pretense at giving an independent view of political events. Christopher K. Robinson, whose company had printed the *Argus* until the paper acquired its own plant, began to publish the *Independent Clarion* in 1914. To distinguish itself from the *Argus*, the *Clarion* stressed its political independence from the Republican Party. Some people speculated that Robinson, who seems to have been a contentious character, started the *Clarion* in a fit of pique when the *Argus* stopped using his printing company. During the five years that he ran the *Independent Clarion*, Robinson's muckraking style angered many in the community, including his wife. In 1919 she sued for divorce, and at the same time Robinson was sued for libel. When his business partners, fearing more legal problems, withdrew their support, Robinson was forced to shut the *Clarion* down. Although a group of businessmen made another attempt to publish the paper in 1923 the venture was not successful, and in 1925 the *Clarion* went out of business for good.[7]

Was John Bird Wilkins the editor of this feisty and short-lived newspaper? That afternoon in the St. Louis County Library, I found a lengthy *Argus* article describing a Christmas party given by C. K. Robinson and his wife for the *Clarion*'s employees in 1915. Although many of the guests are listed by name, my great-grandfather is not mentioned. But he seems to have had some connection with the paper. According to a 1923 *Argus* article, when Bird's son Samuel was a young boy he worked as an apprentice for the *Clarion*.[8] In his obituary John Bird is described as the *Clarion*'s "assistant editor."[9] Perhaps he contributed an occasional article or interview? Given Bird's intellect and obvious gift for words, it's easy to imagine that Robinson's paper would have welcomed an occasional contribution from my great-grandfather.

John Bird's city directory and census entries also lend support to the claim that he worked for the *Clarion* in at least some capacity. In 1919 he is listed in the St. Louis city directory as "Howard B. Wilkins, laborer." But by 1920 my great-grandfather is able to list himself as "Howard B. Wilkins, newspaper editor."[10]

After several hours spent poring over microfilm in the St. Louis County Library, John and I were eager to get out and see The Ville for ourselves. I carefully noted down the addresses I had found in the city directory for "Howard B. Wilkins" and family. Then we left the library, gassed up the rental car, and drove into the city along Martin Luther King Drive.

When my great-grandfather lived here in the 1920s and 1930s this street, then called Easton Avenue, was bustling with commerce. Joe Wolff's Shoe Company, "the place to buy shoes for the family," stood in the 4100 block. A photographer's shop, a tailor's, and a dry-cleaning establishment were located nearby. The Singer Company sold sewing machines at number 4257, while the Easton-Taylor Newsstand offered candies, cigarettes, magazines, greeting cards, and books for sale two blocks down. Dr. Aldrich Brooks, a black dentist, built an office building to house his dental practice in the 4200 block. In that same block the Elleardsville Financial Corporation, started by eight African American businessmen, was available to help local residents acquire loans to build or repair their homes.[11]

As John and I drove slowly down King Drive, surveying the neighborhood, there was little sign of present-day commercial activity. Many of the buildings had been torn down or boarded up while others simply stood empty, a mute and melancholy testament to the neighborhood's neglected status. The headquarters of the *St. Louis Argus* occupied the middle of the 4500 block. At the height of its popularity, the *Argus* had been one of the most important black newspapers in the country. But as desegregation opened opportunities for African Americans to work outside of the black community, many historically black institutions languished.[12] Both the *Argus* building and its surrounding neighborhood reflected this downward spiral. The building's windows were covered with burglar bars; a glass panel in its front door had been replaced by plywood.

After stopping to snap a few pictures, John and I drove on, eager to see if the home where my great-grandfather had lived for many of his years in St. Louis still existed. After making a U-turn on King Drive, we drove southeast and turned left onto 42nd Street. There were vacant lots everywhere. Some blocks had only one or two houses left standing, but other blocks showed signs of revitalization, their houses sporting wrought-iron fences and well-maintained yards.

The block where John Bird Wilkins and his family once lived was quiet and peaceful. Unlike many other blocks in the neighborhood, most of the buildings on this part of Labadie Avenue remained intact. Small brick bungalows with covered porches lined each side of the street. My husband pulled the car to the curb, and I got out to look for number 4216, only to find that the house where my great-grandfather once lived had been torn down. Still, the ground remained. He had walked here, perhaps planting flowers in the front yard or playing with his younger children in the backyard. As I contemplated the overgrown lot where his house once stood, I tried to imagine what life in that home might have been like.

In 1919 John Bird was living at 4216 Labadie Avenue under the name of Howard B. Wilkins. By this time many of his children with Lena Murphy had left home. Their son Howard was a laborer, McKinley was a janitor, and Everett worked as a mail clerk. In 1914, in Little Rock, Arkansas, John Bird and Lena had given birth to their last child, a boy they named William.[13] Their son Samuel, who had apprenticed with the *Clarion* as a boy, was now in his early twenties. A graduate of Shorter College in Little Rock, Samuel trained as a linotypist and now worked at the *Argus*. On March 30, 1923, the paper wrote a short feature on the boy, describing him as "the youngest colored Linotype Operator in the country." After letting their readers know that Samuel, despite his young age, was already married, the *Argus* article then mentioned that his father, "Dr. J. B. Wilkins, is a well known theologican [sic] of St. Louis and president of the Business Men's Bible Training School."[14]

The Bible Training School, another one of my great-grandfather's ventures, was never listed in the St. Louis business directory. It is possible the school was less of an official "school" and more of an informal study group that met at John Bird's Labadie Avenue home. Although he does not seem to have been officially associated with any particular church, my great-grandfather did speak as a guest pastor on at least one occasion. On July 2, 1921, the following article appeared in the *Chicago Defender*'s column "Our Weekly Sermon":

Religion Is Love
By Rev. J. B. Wilkins, Cairo, ILL.
(sent by Mrs. W. C. Simmons)
RELIGION IS LOVE. It is a creative force that demands of us completeness. It is the motive in God's creation. It is all that He demands of man. It is that which gives to us the highest conception of our relations to God and to creation. It sweetly calls us ever on toward fairer lands and upward to the lofty peaks of glorified vision where stands the cross "towering o'er the wrecks of Time." If we have failed in wisdom if a tangle comes in the web of life Love smooths it out for us. All things can be accomplished by its aid and kept right by its power. Love does not have to see to know that everything is all right. It sees through clouds of our ignorance and discovers in us a beauty which it alone creates. It completes life. If we have been unkind Love puts itself into the gap. If there has been a harsh word Love transmutes it, changes it into an excuse for us. It awakens the song that sleeps in every heart, and it is Love's fingers that touch the chords of the instrument which leads the orchestra of the spheres. It smites the sealed fountains and they flow in bubbling brooks that leap into the rivers that bring joy and fertility to parched lands.[15]

John Bird Wilkins may have been a man of many identities, a bigamist, and a congenital liar, but for me his sermons ring true, expressing profound truths in a clear and convincing manner. I hope the congregation in Cairo, a small Illinois town on the Mississippi River, appreciated his address that summer Sunday. Perhaps my great-grandfather was even invited to return. If so, however, I could find no record of the sermon he might have given.

As I continued to absorb the atmosphere on the street where John Bird once lived, I wondered whether he had ever run across J. Ernest or his brothers around the neighborhood. Like many black communities of the time, The Ville was small, less than one square mile.[16] Given the limited employment opportunities available to blacks at the time, it seems inevitable that Bird's two sets of children would have come in contact with each other. J. Ernest's older brothers, Aravelle and Byrd, were both living in the area in 1920, working as mail clerks for the railroad. Just like my grandfather, John Bird and Lena's oldest son, Everett, served in the 809th Pioneers during the war.[17]

J. Ernest was such a brilliant student that he finished his secondary education at Lincoln Institute an entire year early.[18] Before heading off to college at the University of Illinois, he worked briefly at a normal school that Lincoln had opened on Cottage Avenue, in The Ville. In a picture taken of the Sumner Teaching College's faculty that year, my grandfather stands in the front row, sporting an elegant tweed suit and looking very professorial.[19]

The teaching college was located in the heart of The Ville, less than a mile from John Bird's home. Had J. Ernest ever bumped into his father at the movies or while shopping for groceries along Easton Avenue? After he went away to the University of Illinois in 1914, J. Ernest stayed with his brothers Aravelle and Byrd during his summer vacations, working to earn money for the next year's tuition. The brothers lived only two miles away from their father and his other family.

J. Ernest and his brothers were probably aware that, in October 1922, John Bird's sons Samuel and Theodore were involved in a serious scandal. According to the *Chicago Defender,* the pair were arrested for stealing bonus checks intended for army veterans. The thefts were discovered when a former soldier wrote to inquire about his missing bonus and was informed that the check had allegedly been signed by him and endorsed over to "S. B. Wilkins." Once the forgeries were discovered, it wasn't long before Samuel and Theodore were arrested on felony charges.[20] It seems that Samuel, at least, did not spend very much time in jail, because less than six months later, he is working as "the fastest colored linotypist" for the *Argus.*[21]

By the time of this scandal, my grandfather had just started his legal career. As someone who was beginning to make a name for himself among Chicago's light-skinned elite, J. Ernest would have found the whole situation deeply embarrassing. It's likely my grandfather would have seen the arrest of his two half brothers as further confirmation of John Bird's failings both as a father and as a human being.

After my grandfather's graduation from law school, his name began to appear in the papers. In 1922 he was elected Grand Keeper of Records for his fraternity, Kappa Alpha Psi. In 1929 J. Ernest was awarded the Laurel Wreath, Kappa Alpha Psi's highest honor.[22] Both these events were widely covered in the black press. My guess is that John Bird (who was, after all, a self-proclaimed "newspaperman") was well aware of his boy's success.

Did father and son ever reconcile? It would be nice to think that sometime later in life, perhaps as adults, they were able to sit down and talk. But it doesn't seem likely. Aunt Marjory, a colorful if not always reliable source, used to tell the following story: "J. Ernest's father was a ne'er-do-well and wanted nothing to do with J. Ernest when the boy was little. But when your grandfather started to get well known, his father changed his tune and tried to visit him in Chicago. Now that J. Ernest was doing well, the old man wanted to get back in touch. He even went by and knocked on your grandfather's door. But J. Ernest refused to see him. And that was it. They never spoke after that."

As John and I continued to absorb the atmosphere along Labadie Avenue, the sun, which had been broiling down on us for much of the day, ducked behind a cloud. A screen door banged shut somewhere further down the block. John put his arm around me and gave me a gentle squeeze. "We should probably get moving if you want to see the rest of The Ville today," he said. I nodded, and after taking one final snapshot, got back in our rental car.

The next place I wanted to see was at 4407 Kennerly Avenue, where John Bird Wilkins had spent the last eight years of his life. On this block, as on many of the streets in The Ville, several houses had been razed and John Bird's former home was now a vacant lot. But there were also signs of renewed life in the neighborhood. A large modern church stood directly across the street. Families relaxing on their front porches eyed us curiously. The sight of a balding white man and a light-skinned black woman emerging from a rental car to stare reverently at an empty lot was definitely an attention-grabber.

Before I could worry too much about the spectacle we were providing for the locals, John called out, "Carolyn, look! There's a bird over there! Maybe he's come back to help us."

When it comes to matters of the spirit, I can never be sure whether my husband is being serious. My involvement in the Santeria group had taxed our marriage severely, so I was very careful when referencing the supernatural in John's presence. But sure enough, a robin was hopping about on the ground where my great-grandfather's house once stood.

"Yes, John Bird. I see you," I said to myself. "You're an elusive character, but I am doing my level best to document your story." The bird cocked its head provocatively and stared at me. But when I bent down to take its picture, it flew away. For no logical reason at all, I felt the presence of my ancestors as my husband and I got back into the car and drove away.

The next stop on our list was Antioch Baptist Church, where John Bird's funeral had been held. Founded in 1878, Antioch is the oldest church in The Ville, and its building dominated the corner of North Market Street. A green indoor-outdoor carpet covered the steps leading to the church's entrance, while a sign in front announced the sermon topic for the following Sunday. In 1915, when my great-grandfather was living nearby, Antioch Baptist Church had a membership roll of five hundred people and was in the process of raising money for a new sanctuary.[23] The church's size and prestige would have drawn John Bird and Lena to it like a magnet.

Lena may have been a fairly regular member. However, John Bird had once been in charge of his own large church. It is difficult to imagine him sitting in a back pew for too many Sundays, listening to someone else's preaching. But we do know that my great-grandfather visited the church on at least one occasion. A brief blurb in the *Argus* on March 10, 1916, notes that "Rev. H. B. Wilkins, associate editor of the *Clarion*," worshipped at Antioch Baptist Church and was scheduled to speak at the evening service the following Sunday.[24]

Although no longer the charismatic figure he once had been, John Bird continued to preach and teach into his late seventies. In 1927 he returned to

Bethesda Baptist Church in Chicago to preach at its fortieth anniversary celebration. Interviewed by Evangeline Roberts from the *Chicago Defender,* my
great-grandfather was as flamboyant as ever. Now calling himself Dr. J. B.
Wilkins, he described himself as an "author, lecturer and psychologist." In this
interview, he gave himself a medical degree from Jefferson Medical College
and claimed to have been the third black man to graduate from Harvard. And,
in keeping with the day's headlines (the psychopathic murderers Leopold and
Loeb were receiving nationwide publicity), John Bird also claimed to have
"prepared the psychological evaluations used by renowned defense attorney
Clarence Darrow" in a recent Chicago criminal case.[25]

And yet, mixed right in with his bogus resume and shameless self-promotion,
my great-grandfather continued to expound a surprisingly modern religious
philosophy: "My system of theology deals with the subject in reference to the
part the Christian man is to play in this world. I am trying to deal with religion
as a means to an end. It is my desire to show the effect of religion on the individual and what good results from being a Christian, not after death, but now!"
Reflecting back on his controversial career as Bethesda's pastor forty years ago
John Bird stated, "I was a consistent meddler in public affairs and took time off
from singing and praying to look about me and see what was going on. I began
to study the emotions of our people. I was interested in knowing whether real
religion had anything to do with emotion, or whether emotion had anything
to do with real religion."[26]

Although my great-grandfather would live another nine years, this 1927 *Defender* article is the last time I was able to find him written up in the press. On
August 6, 1938, John Bird Wilkins suffered a heart attack and died at 10:35 that
evening at St. Mary's Hospital in St. Louis. According to his death certificate,
my great-grandfather was eighty-seven years old.

In classic John Bird Wilkins fashion, the two obituaries published to announce his death give conflicting biographical information. In the *Chicago
Defender,* he is described as "Rev. J. D. [*sic*] Wilkins, minister and teacher." According to this obituary, he was ordained in Little Rock, Arkansas, in 1870 and
befriended Frederick Douglass while attending Howard University. He worked
for Horace Greeley while a college student and edited the *New Citizen* in Browns-
ville, Tennessee.[27] As usual, most of these claims do not hold up to close scrutiny. Horace Greeley, the famous newspaper editor, died in 1872. He would
have been on his last legs, in New York, during the time that John Bird was sup-
posedly a college student at Howard University, in Washington, D.C. It seems
unlikely that my great-grandfather could have worked for Greeley and gone to
Howard at the same time. Nor is my great-grandfather mentioned anywhere in
the 413 pages of Robert Chadwell Williams's biography, *Horace Greeley: Champion of American Freedom.*[28]

Howard University, like the many other colleges John Bird claimed he attended, has no record of his ever having been a student. And he certainly was not ordained in Little Rock in 1870. As we know, in 1870, my great-grandfather was living in Oxford, Mississippi, and did not come to Little Rock until 1893. By the time he arrived in Little Rock, John Bird had already worked as a Baptist minister in both St. Paul and Chicago.

John Bird's other obituary, published in the *St. Louis Argus,* is longer and somewhat more accurate, though still riddled with questionable facts. Here, my great-grandfather is a graduate of Gammon Theological Seminary and Yale University. As usual, neither Yale nor Gammon has any record of his having been a student there. This obituary, most likely written from information submitted by Lena or one of her children, neatly avoids any reference to John Bird's earlier life in Little Rock, Arkansas, in Oxford, Mississippi, or in Chicago. Instead the article simply states that John Bird Wilkins and Lena Murphy had been living in St. Louis since 1909. We know this to be untrue on several counts, not the least of which is that the U.S. census data confirm that Bird and his family were living in Drew County, Arkansas, in 1910. Not surprisingly, this obituary also fails to mention John Bird's relationship with Susie Douthit. However, the *Argus* article does mention each of John Bird's seventeen children by name, including my grandfather, "Atty J. Ernest Wilkins."[29]

As John and I took one last look at Antioch Baptist Church, I imagined my great-grandfather's funeral cortege as it wound its way toward Washington Park Cemetery. Were there many cars? John Bird was at least eighty-seven when he died. Perhaps many of the people who had known him best had already passed on. Most likely Lena Murphy was there and, hopefully, many of their children. I would bet money, though, that my grandfather J. Ernest Wilkins did not attend.

The digital chime of my cell phone broke into my thoughts. It was Ethel Porter's grandson Chris Wright. We had been playing phone tag all day, trying to set up a time when we could get together. He had some old family pictures he wanted to show me. We made a date to meet in the lounge of my hotel the next night after he got off from work.

As John piloted our rental car away from the city, I permitted myself a small moment of silent relief. After traveling over a thousand miles and spending hundreds of dollars, my worst nightmare had been that I would leave St. Louis with nothing to show for my efforts. But now that I had a definite date set to meet Chris, I would at least have some new pictures to take home with me. Perhaps, if things worked out right, Chris Wright might even have a picture of my slave ancestor, Aunt Marjory's mighty mythical Jeremiah. Bit by bit, everything was beginning to fall into place.

Aunt Sarah

Chapter Eleven

Farmington, Missouri

As John and I merged onto Route I-55 the next morning, a light drizzle misted the windshield of our rental car. By the time we pulled into Farmington ninety minutes later, the rain was coming down in sheets. Gusts of wind threw water up onto the windshield and rippled the puddles accumulating in the street. I had hoped to be able to get a feel for my grandfather's birthplace by taking a walk around the town, but in this weather a leisurely stroll down Main Street was out of the question.

Fortunately, we had also made indoor plans. According to my trusty researcher, Mariah Cooper, Farmington Public Library maintained a significant archive of historic local documents. Perhaps one of these documents would shed more light on my grandfather's early life. At the very least I hoped to find proof that John Bird had married either Susie Douthit or Lena Murphy while in Farmington.

After finding a space for our car in the library's parking lot, we sprinted through the rain up a short flight of stairs, stepped breathlessly into the main reading room, and stopped short. A small group of children sat in a circle around their teacher at one end of the room. On the other side, in a small corner, stood a few bookshelves holding general books on Missouri history.

"I don't know that we're going to find much here," I muttered half under my breath. "This place is *tiny.*"

"Don't give up yet," John replied. "Remember, I used to be a librarian myself. Looks can be deceiving. Let me talk to them and see if I can get a sense of what they've got."

While I stood by the front door dripping water from my raincoat, John bustled off to find a librarian. A few minutes later he was back with a young man in tow. "What we want to see is in the library's genealogy room," John announced triumphantly. "Carolyn, meet Travis. He'll take us down there now."

Travis Trokey, a dark-haired man who looked to be no older than thirty, smiled obligingly and led us around to the back of the building and down a flight of stairs to the basement, turning on the lights along the way. In the basement's small foyer stood a card catalogue, several drawers of microfilm and two microfilm readers. Stopping at a large glass door, Travis produced a key and unlocked the door with a flourish.

"This is our genealogy room," he announced. "I think you will be able to find a lot of information about your Farmington ancestors here. Be sure to let me know if you need any more help."

The room was spacious, and the walls were lined on three sides with books about Farmington's history. Against the fourth wall, a librarian's work desk was piled high with papers.

"We have editions of the *Farmington News* going back to 1883, as well as many county probate documents and census records," Travis told us. "We even have some slave schedules."

After making sure we were properly settled, Travis took a seat at his desk and began to tap away at the computer keys. Except for Travis, John and I had the room to ourselves. It was time to go to work. Spreading our things out on the large wooden worktable in the center of the room, I consulted my list of questions:

(1) Among all the Farmington histories that lined the shelves, was there any mention of either John Bird or J. Ernest Wilkins? What about Susie Douthit or Lena Murphy?

(2) Were there any records that could prove that John Bird Wilkins had married either Susie Douthit or Lena Murphy in Farmington?

(3) What had life been like for black folks in Farmington in 1894 when my grandfather was born? Where did they work and play? Where did they go to church and to school?

(4) Was there anything I could discover in J. Ernest's early life that might help me to understand him better? Perhaps if I could truly understand his childhood, I might be able to comprehend why he had driven himself so hard and why he felt he had to resign his position at the Labor Department.

As had become our pattern, John and I divided the research work between us. He scanned the library's holdings for references to African Americans, and to Wilkinses in particular. I concentrated on learning about Farmington's history.

William Murphy, the town's founding father, was a Kentucky native who led a party of four across the Mississippi River in search of new land in 1798. After landing in St. Genevieve, the men traveled west and staked their claims in the location of present-day Farmington. Murphy died on his way back home, but his three sons returned with their families to settle permanently in the area in the spring of 1800. When the United States bought Missouri from the French as a part of the Louisiana Purchase in 1803, the town of Farmington became the seat of St. Francois County. In 1851 a plank road was built right through the center of Farmington to connect the river town of St. Genevieve to the ore-rich mountains to the west.[1]

Despite its favorable location, Farmington's population remained small. In 1885, when John Bird Wilkins lived there, the town had less than fifteen hundred inhabitants. The town did not get its first automobile until 1900 and did not build its first concrete road until 1919.[2]

As I pored over the history books, I couldn't help but notice that they barely mentioned the town's slaves. Frowning and beginning to grumble to myself, I plowed on. The next book on the shelf was a book put together by the staff at the library called *Farmington, Missouri: The First 200 Years.* From the census data I'd read, I knew that roughly one Farmington citizen out of ten had been African American at the turn of the last century. Surely this hefty volume would contain some useful information about what life was like for the town's black population? There were scores of vintage photographs, a beautifully reproduced town map from 1880, a time line of significant dates in Farmington history, and pages of detailed information about the town's citizens.

With increasing desperation I paged through the book hunting for some mention of the town's black history. I read about P. T. Pigg, the founder of the *Farmington News.* I read about the family that founded Tetley's Jewelry Store and saw pictures of Laakman's Drug Store, the Burnett Meat Market, Lloyd and Mayberry Stables, and the Brown Hotel. There were photos of the Farmington High School football team, the 1902 offices of the telephone company, and a great 1900 photo of downtown Farmington's Washington Street. With the exception of a few sentences on slavery in the book's Civil War chapter, it seemed Farmington's first two hundred years had occurred without the contribution of a single African American.

Paging through the book with increasing urgency, I came across a small profile on Ethelean Cayce. During slavery, Ethelean's family had belonged to one of the county's largest slave owners, the merchant and mill owner Milton P. Cayce. Her grandfather, Jeter Cayce, had somehow managed to save $450 while he was enslaved. At the end of the Civil War, Cayce used his savings to buy a large tract of land near what is the center of Farmington today. On this land he built a homestead for his family. In her interview for this profile, Ethelean Cayce spoke with pride of her family's roots. When asked whether she had ever experienced racism in town, she replied, "Farmington has always been good to colored people."

While still a young girl, Ethelean began to work as a domestic servant. At first she hated the work and wanted to quit. But her mother told her, "Go back. You'll learn to like it."

The article went on to describe with a surprising lack of irony how Ethelean subsequently "went on to help many families with various household chores." The article concluded, "It's people like Ethelean who continue to demonstrate the characteristics of the men and women who first settled the area."[3]

I am a child of the 1960s. I find it difficult to believe that Ethelean Cayce was being absolutely candid with her white interviewers. And I couldn't help wondering why my grandfather—a Farmington native and the first black Assistant Secretary of Labor in U.S. history—was not mentioned in this book. Granted, he had not lived in Farmington since he was a teenager, but he had been a native son, with accomplishments at least as significant as Ms. Cayce's.

I continued to roam the shelves. I was searching with increasing urgency for a book that could tell me the story of Farmington's black folks. John, meanwhile, was busy checking the St. Francois County marriage records.

"There are no marriages listed for 1885–1900 under the name of John Bird Wilkins, Bird Wilkins, or Howard Wilkins in St. Francois County," he reported, removing his glasses to massage the bridge of his nose. "I've checked and double-checked."

"Thanks, hon. That's what Mariah Cooper had suspected. Now we know for sure. How are you feeling?" By this point, we had been at it for over three hours, and I was beginning to despair of finding out anything useful about my grandfather's early life. My husband, however, when he is doing research, has the tenacity of a pit bull.

"I'm fine," he smiled, replacing his glasses. "I'm going to scan the newspapers on microfilm and see if they have anything useful." He ambled out to the foyer and began loading microfilm into the reader. I hadn't said anything to John, but truth was, I was getting tired.

"If I don't find anything in an hour," I told myself, "I'm going to give up." I shot up a quick prayer to the ancestors. "Please help me find what I am supposed to find here," I whispered. "We've come such a long way."

I got up to take one more look at the books in the Local History section. Then I saw it. Tucked away at the end of a row of books I had already gone over at least twice was a thin sheaf of Xeroxed pages, looking more like an eighth grader's term paper than an actual book. Its typed cover read, "African American History in Farmington: This material has been compiled and donated to the Farmington Public Library by Faye Sitzes."

Bingo! I'd hit pay dirt.

"John!" I shouted, forgetting for a moment where I was. (Fortunately Travis, our helpful librarian, had long since vacated his desk.) "I've found it! A book on the black history of Farmington." I rushed to the Xerox machine and carefully photocopied every page. Then, as the rain splattered gently against the small window over Travis's desk, I sat down at the long wooden table and began to read.

When she arrived in Farmington in 1802, Sarah Barton Murphy brought two African Americans with her. In Marcus Kirkland's 1965 article "The Early History of Farmington," the pair are described only as "a Negro woman and a boy."[4] Since the Murphy family had roots in Tennessee, where slavery was an established part of life, it's likely that the pair were Murphy's slaves.

Although Missouri fought on the side of the Union in the Civil War, it remained a slave state. By the time of the 1860 census, slaves represented an important part of Farmington's labor force, providing manual labor for the local farms, mills, and lead mines. Slaves assisted the local doctor on his rounds and worked in town as clerks, handymen, and domestic workers. The buying and selling of human beings was a common sight in Farmington.[5] Estate sales at which slaves were auctioned were held on the courthouse steps at the beginning of each new year.

By the time my grandfather was growing up in 1900, slavery had been abolished, but racial segregation was the norm in every aspect of daily life. In 1870 the town built an elementary school for its white students, and in 1896 Farmington High School graduated its first class. But although Farmington's 358 black citizens constituted roughly 10 percent of the town's total population, these facilities were off-limits for black students.

Along with the rest of the town's African American children, my grandfather attended the Douglas Street School, a rough two-room schoolhouse on the far side of town. When Dayse Baker, one of the school's two teachers, began at Douglas in 1903, seventy-five pupils were being taught in two rooms. Grades one through four had class in the first room, while a second teacher taught grades five through eight in the other.[6] As a teacher myself, I couldn't begin to imagine trying to function in such a crowded environment.

Fifty years later, Baker described what her job had been like to a reporter from the *St. Louis Post-Dispatch.* How was she able to attend to so many pupils, the amazed interviewer asked. "In multi-grade schools in those days, the grade ahead taught the one behind," Miss Baker responded.[7] The fact that anyone learned anything at all in this environment is a testament to the remarkable nature of Miss Baker's teaching skills and to the value placed on education by Farmington's African American community.

When J. Ernest was growing up, Farmington's black community provided plenty of role models for the qualities he would later exemplify. These were hardworking people with a stoic sense of self-reliance. They didn't whine, they didn't complain, nor did they let racism faze them. If Farmington's black community wanted something done, they didn't wait for outsiders to do it for them, they simply handled it themselves.

Sometime in the mid 1870s, a charismatic pastor named Christopher Tayes began to talk to blacks in the area about building their own church. Legend has it that Tayes walked as many as twenty miles daily, soliciting funds for his cause.

Tayes's dream was realized in 1877 when St. Paul Methodist Episcopal Church was built on a small lot purchased from Jeter Cayce.[8] St. Paul's congregation took pride in their church, having built most of it themselves. They sat on pews made by local carpenters and took communion from a table covered by handmade cloth. The windows were framed by lace curtains that had been sewn by church members. My grandfather would have spent many an hour inside the church during his childhood, warmed by a potbellied stove in the winter months.

In an extensive interview given in 1998, church member Ethelean Cayce recalled, "My family always was strong in faith. When I was a child we went to church three times on Sunday. Sunday school, then 11 a.m. services and again for the evening service at 7 p.m. That's all we did on Sundays."[9]

Many of Farmington's black citizens attended St. Paul's. Dayse Baker, the elementary schoolteacher and author of weekly "Farmington News" columns in the *Argus*, taught in the Sunday school. Ethelean Cayce, whose grandfather had sold the land to the congregation, played the piano and organ there. My great-grandmother Susie's father, Hilliard Douthit, was one of the original founders of the church.[10] J. Ernest's older brother Charles would go on to become a Methodist minister. I am sure my grandfather's deep and abiding connection to the Methodist church springs from this early formative environment.

Susie lived in different locations around the Farmington area during her lifetime. When she was a child, her parents rented a home near the edge of town. While raising J. Ernest and his four siblings, she lived in a house on Cayce Avenue. Later still, she owned her own home on West Street.[11]

Now that I had read up on Farmington's black history, I was ready to get out and see some of the town. As I stood up and stretched, I took a peek through the window. The rain was beginning to lighten. It was still drizzling, but the clouds were breaking. Armed with an umbrella, I would be able to take my walk around the town after all. When I stepped into the foyer, John was rewinding a roll of microfilm.

Over the gentle whirring of the machine, I called out, "Babe, I'm tired and hungry. What do you say to a change of scenery? I'd like to grab some lunch and then drive around town a bit. I need to take some pictures before the sun goes down."

"Sounds good," John replied, slipping the rewound reel of microfilm back into its box. "I've scanned through the newspapers here. There's very little about black people in here, though."

"I know. I think the most important articles are in the clipping file I copied. Let's get some lunch."

After packing up and thanking Travis Trokey for his help, we left the library and drove to Burger King. By the time we finished lunch, the rain had stopped and the sky was clearing. Small shafts of sunlight poked their way through the clouds. It was time to go exploring.

The first thing we discovered was that all three of the houses where Susie Douthit once lived had been torn down. The street numbers on Cayce Street had been changed, and a large nursing home now occupied the entire block. West Street, where Susie had owned a home in 1930, was little more than a back alley. Large houses faced away from West Street toward the parallel streets on either side. When Susie lived here, she was working as a laundress. Perhaps her employer occupied one of the larger houses nearby?

Feeling thwarted, I suggested to John that we drive out to the cemetery to look at my great-grandmother's grave. As we drove through the peaceful, winding streets to the eastern edge of town, the scenery became more rural. The lots and the houses were larger, the satellite TV dishes in their backyards giving mute testimony to Farmington's distance from the big city. Horses grazed in the late afternoon sunlight. Now that it wasn't raining, the air was soft and vaguely tropical. Perhaps because it was still only the middle of the day, the streets were empty. It felt like John and I had the town to ourselves.

After we had driven for several minutes, John eased the car onto the shoulder of the road.

"Are you sure this is the right way?" he asked.

I pulled out the detailed map that Travis had given us in the library. "Yep. It's on Old Colony Road. It says so right here." I poked my index finger on the paper. "Let's just keep driving. If we don't hit it in the next fifteen minutes, we'll turn around."

Looking dubious, John started the car and pulled back on to the street. Though I said nothing to John, I was really enjoying our cruise in the country. Even if we never found the cemetery, I could gain a valuable sense of what living in this small town might have been like in 1894. The vista was beautiful and must have been truly amazing then. Rolling hills and green farmland stretched in all directions, and when I rolled my car window down, the air outside smelled like clover.

John, however, was getting frustrated. He's a goal-oriented guy and hates to get lost. To keep him distracted, I told him the story of how Colored Masonic Cemetery was created.

In 1902 twenty-three of Farmington's black Masons formed a graveyard association to purchase land for a cemetery. They raised money and purchased the site on Colony Road. They even built the road that led to the land. Among these men were the town's most prominent black citizens, including several members of Ethelean Cayce's family and Lewis Murphy, Lena's father. According to the association's by-laws, the wife, children, or direct descendants of any person buried there could also be buried in the cemetery free of charge.[12] Susie Douthit Wilkins, three of her brothers, and J. Ernest's brother Byrd are all interred there.

"It always blows me away how self-reliant these people were," John remarked after I had told him the story.

"I know what you mean," I replied. "In those days no one expected anyone to do anything for them. They knew if they wanted a decent place to bury their families they'd have to do it themselves. So they raised money, bought the land, built a road, and gave themselves a cemetery." As John continued to look out for road signs, I shook my head in admiration. "You don't see too much of that sort of thing anymore," I told him. "Nowadays, people complain and wait for the government or someone else to fix the problem."

"At least now the government feels some responsibility to help African Americans. Back then, few white people cared if blacks had access to services."

I sighed. Of course, John was right. As usual. "Look," I cried. "That's it, on the left."

At the top of the next rise stood a small plot of land surrounded by a chain-link fence. John pulled over and turned off the engine. As the car ticked down, the only other sound I could hear was the sighing of the wind. Looking for a way inside, I walked around to the front of the cemetery. The front gate was locked, but there was a hole in the chain-link fencing along the side. Clutching the bouquet of flowers I had brought along, I wriggled through.

A rutted dirt road led straight through the cemetery, lined on both sides by modest headstones. The grass was wet from the recent rain. It had been mowed recently and smelled sweet. On the right side of the graveyard, not far from the entrance, stood a headstone inscribed "Wilkins." Susie, her son Byrd and his wife, Mayme Swink, were buried there. I couldn't help but contrast the condition of this cemetery to the one where John Bird was interred. There were definite signs that this place was still being cared for. The location was beautiful and imbued with a deep sense of peace.

As I laid my flowers on the grave, I said a prayer. "Dear God, bring peace to my ancestors. Thank you so much, Susie Douthit Wilkins, for the life you lived. I know you struggled against many obstacles and must have felt abandoned and alone on many occasions. But now you are at peace. From across the years I salute you and thank you for being my ancestor. You have not been forgotten."

Now, there was just one more place I wanted to see. According to the articles I had just read in the library, Colored Hall and the first site of St. Paul

Methodist Episcopal Church were both located on Jefferson Street, close to the center of town. Much of Farmington had changed in the 115 years since my grandfather was born there. But perhaps at least one of these buildings was still standing?

According to one of the articles I had read, "Professor" Bird J. Wilkins had organized a group called the Colored Working Men's Association to build a community center in 1885. Known in the community as Colored Hall, the building became home to the black Knights of Pythias, the black Masons, and three different black churches at one time or another. Another article written about the building in the late 1990s included a picture of a small wooden structure and stated that the building was now the home of the Native Woods Gallery.[13] But as we pulled the car up to the curb, all that remained of Colored Hall was a flight of concrete steps and a railing. It was a sad sight. I deeply wished someone had at least put a historical marker there to mark the spot. Boston, where John and I live, is littered with historical markers. They help to put things in context, to remind future generations that although time has moved on, history happened here, on this very spot.

Kitty-corner to the ruins, however, was the building where the St. Paul Methodist Church congregation had once met. The Knights of Pythias had purchased the building, and it seemed in relatively good condition. Although it had been remodeled several times, its distinctive sloped roof and hexagonal side windows still gave it a church-like quality.

After walking around and taking some photos, I got back in the car where John sat idling the engine and contentedly puffing his pipe. It had been a long day, and we were both very tired. Soon it would be dark, and we still had a two-hour drive to get back to our hotel. It was time to hit the road. As we pulled away from the curb, I took a last look at the ruins of Colored Hall. I had only spent an afternoon here, but after my visit to Farmington I felt connected to my Wilkins heritage in a deeper and more intimate way. Although there had been occasions in my life when people mistook me for a white girl, I was now feeling a lot more certain about who I really was.

It was rush hour. The closer we got to the outskirts of St. Louis, the thicker the traffic became. Hemmed in by a sixteen wheeler on one side and a mammoth SUV on the other, we inched our way along Route I-55, peering anxiously at each road sign to make sure we hadn't passed our exit. John hates driving in heavy traffic and was mumbling profanities under his breath. I was doing my best to pretend I didn't hear them when my cell phone rang. It was Chris Wright, Ethel Porter's grandson. The day before, I had made tentative plans to get together with him some time this evening. I had gotten so wrapped up in my Farmington trip I had completely forgotten our appointment.

"Hey Carolyn, are we still on for tonight? I'm running a bit behind at work, but I could be at your hotel by seven."

I was exhausted and had been looking forward to a long hot bath and a night of mindless TV. But the opportunity to meet Chris and look over the old family pictures he had was not to be missed. He was a busy guy and if I cancelled, who knew when or if we would be able to get together again.

"Sure, Chris. That would be great. We've been in Farmington all day but we're just passing the airport right now. I should be back at the hotel in plenty of time to meet you."

Promising to call me if he got delayed, Chris hung up. From the little he had told me about himself, I gathered that he worked at St. Louis University Hospital. An emergency surgery had been scheduled for the afternoon, and he sounded at least as tired as I was. As John eased the car down the exit ramp toward our hotel, I had to smile to myself. Those ancestors, I thought to myself. They will really get you in some unusual predicaments. In the past three days I had spent several hundred dollars to walk around graveyards and look at the ruins of old buildings. Now, despite being totally exhausted, I was about to meet with a total stranger.

Chris Wright arrived an hour late, but I didn't mind. For at least an hour I had been able to lie on my hotel bed and stare blankly at the TV without thinking about anything. I had known that the trip to Farmington would be important. I'd had no idea how emotionally draining it would be.

As Chris and I approached each other in the hotel lobby, we appraised each other cautiously. We were, after all, total strangers. In this age of identity theft and random violent crime, one can't be too careful. But as soon as I got up close, I could see that Dr. James Christopher Wright was no stranger. In some strange way, although we had never met before and might never meet again, we were family. After an awkward hug, Chris and I settled ourselves at a cocktail table in the corner of the hotel lounge farthest away from the TV. While a motley crew of inebriated businessmen munched peanuts and stared fixedly at the Cardinals game, Chris opened a large plastic storage crate filled to the brim with pictures, each one individually wrapped in a Ziploc baggie.

For some reason, when talking to him on the phone, I had imagined Chris to be an older man. But as I watched him over the small table, I saw he was in fact younger than me, very handsome, and like myself with a light complexion. Though cordial, Dr. Chris had clearly had a rough day. He had come straight from work and was still in his blue hospital scrubs. There were serious bags under his auburn eyes, and worry lines around his smile. I tried to make small talk, but Chris got right down to business.

"As you can see, I've got a ton of pictures here." Carefully, he began to remove pictures from the crate and spread them out on the table. "I don't know exactly what you're interested in seeing."

This was the magic moment I had been waiting for. But now it was here, I didn't know quite how to proceed.

"Well," I said slowly. "I know that my Aunt Marjory was Mrs. Porter's great-niece, and that they both had Jeremiah McFarland in their family tree." Then I told Chris an abbreviated version of the story Aunt Marjory used to tell at family gatherings. How Jeremiah had come from Africa, been brought to New York, and sold into slavery in Kentucky to a man named Robinson.

"Well, I don't have any pictures of Jeremiah McFarland. But I do have a picture of his wife, Sarah. She was part Irish and part Native American. She's our earliest ancestor. Would you like to see it?"

"Wow!" I said, my tiredness falling away. "Would I ever! Would you mind if I took a picture of her?"

Chris nodded and began to rummage through his box. He must have had over a hundred pictures in there. "Here she is," he said, carefully unwrapping an old piece of metal. "This is what they call a tintype. They used to print pictures on pieces of metal back in the day."

With trembling hands I took the photo. And across five generations and 150 years, Sarah McFarland looked me squarely in the eye. Unflinching she gazed into the camera, her square jaw set, her long hair pulled back from her face and parted in the center. Her hair seems to be braided, but from the angle the photo was taken it's impossible to be sure. With her high cheekbones and dark eyes, Sarah's Native American ancestry is unmistakable. She's wearing a simple dark colored dress with a high white collar. Around her neck she wears two beaded necklaces. Even at this distance in time, her strength of character comes through. Aunt Marj's great-grandmother was not a woman to be taken lightly.

For the next half hour, Chris pulled photo after photo from his storage crate. Many of them were shots of people from Mrs. Porter's side of the family whom I did not recognize. Chris did not recognize them either. In becoming his family's historian, he was honoring the request of his one-hundred-year-old grandmother. These were her pictures, and just like my Aunt Marjory, Ethel Porter was her family's griot. Chris and I, each in our own way, were merely struggling to preserve the family legacy.

Shortly after celebrating her one hundredth birthday, Mrs. Porter suffered a stroke, Dr. Chris told me. It was doubtful she would recover. With a tear in his eye, Chris told me he felt the end was near. When she received my card at her birthday party, Mrs. Porter insisted that Chris get in touch with me. And now that she was no longer able to speak for herself, Dr. Chris felt it imperative that we get together, despite his busy schedule at the hospital.

The more he told me about Mrs. Porter, the more she reminded me of Aunt Marjory. Like Aunt Marj, Ethel Porter had a long career as a teacher. And like

Aunt Marj, Mrs. Porter was well-known for her generosity. After she retired from teaching, Mrs. Porter raised Chris for a time when his mother was struggling to make ends meet.

"My grandmother was just like that," he told me. "Always helping other people."

It was nearly 9 o'clock now, and I could tell Dr. Chris was getting tired. I had brought my camera to our rendezvous and was trying as best I could to take decent photos of some of the family pictures I recognized. He promised to scan some photos for me later on, but we both knew that, given his busy schedule, other things would soon take precedence. My mother always used to say, "A bird in hand is worth two in the bush." My pictures might not be studio quality, but at least I would have some shots of Sarah to take home with me. After showing me one more wonderful photograph of Aunt Marjory as a young girl, dressed in her finest and riding a Shetland pony, Dr. Chris packed away his collection and stood. The Cardinals game was over. The businessmen had long since gone back to their rooms. We now had the lounge to ourselves.

"Chris, I can't thank you enough," I said. "I know you must be exhausted, and I really appreciate you coming down here to meet me. Next time you come to Boston, please call me. John and I will take you out to a lobster dinner."

After one final hug, Chris picked up his box and walked out of the hotel. Still vibrating from the encounter, I rushed upstairs to download my photos. "We are Fa-mi-ly!" I sang, startling the desk clerk as I walked past. "We are Fa-mi-ly!"

Lucile and Aunt Marj c. 1945

Chapter Twelve

Blackness

After John and I returned home from our St. Louis trip, I wrote up a chronicle of our research for my diary, emailed a copy of Aunt Sarah's picture to everyone in the family, and returned to the rest of my life. I was in the middle of preparing for a concert with my jazz group while at the same time writing a textbook on singing. Although I was still curious to find out about my grandfather's resignation from the Labor Department, I was just too busy to pursue my research any further.

I wasn't the only busy one in the family. My youngest brother, Timothy, was negotiating a billion-dollar deal for his New York law firm. My middle brother, Stephen, was organizing a new sports program for Chicago's public elementary schools. And my brother David, a professor at Harvard Law School, was becoming involved in politics.

While I was channel surfing one night, a familiar sight caught my eye. Displayed on the screen behind an attractive young anchorwoman, my brother David's house was clearly visible. "One of the most watched political candidates in the country sneaked into the Hub for a second time on Tuesday. . . . The senator was in town for one thing and one thing only," the Fox News reporter gushed, "campaign cash." As the reporter continued to describe Barack Obama's fund-raising hopes for the evening, the candidate is shown walking up the sidewalk to my brother's house. David stands near the door to usher Obama inside, firmly closing the door on the camera's prying eye.[1]

Long before Barack Obama became a household name, the Wilkins family had established a friendship with the charismatic senator. For one thing, Obama was a Chicago resident, whose Hyde Park home was located less than a mile from where we had grown up. Obama sent his children to the same private school my brothers and I had attended as kids. And like my father, two of my brothers, and my Uncle John, Barack Obama attended Harvard Law School.

105

When my brother David became a professor there, the candidate's future wife, Michelle, was one of David's favorite students.

If Obama were attacked, the Wilkins family took it personally. In the summer of 2007, the harsh punishment meted out to six black students convicted of fighting with white students in Jena, Louisiana, sparked national outrage. When Obama did not clear his schedule to attend a march supporting the Jena Six, black civil rights icon Jesse Jackson criticized the senator for "acting like he's white." Though Jackson, who had run a losing presidential campaign in 1988, later claimed he did not remember making the remark, the incident received a great deal of media attention.[2]

Jesse Jackson is a political fixture in Chicago, and my brothers and I all voted for him in 1988. But his comments disparaging Obama did not play well with the Wilkins family.

"The man is outrageous," my mother fumed. "Who made him God? He's just trying to drag Barack down in the mud."

David had his own take on Jackson's remarks. "When Jesse Jackson ran, there was no chance at all for a black man to become President. But things are different now. And Barack is different. He's going to make it—just wait and see."

For me, the attack on Obama's "black authenticity" resonated strongly at a personal level. For as long as I could remember I have had to prove my black bona fides to skeptics on both sides of the color line. When I was in high school, some of the other black students accused me of "talking like a white girl." After this incident, I carefully developed two separate vocabularies, one for dealing with white teachers and schoolmates and another that (hopefully) would enable me to be "down with the brothers." Although I loved my high school, I never told black friends from the neighborhood that I went to a private school for fear of being called an "Oreo," that is, someone who is black on the outside but white on the inside. Despite these evasive maneuvers, I was frequently criticized by other blacks for being too "bougie," that is, too at ease with white folks and white culture. When I first arrived at college, many of my soul brothers and sisters did not return my greetings for the first few weeks until they figured out that despite my light skin, I was indeed, one of them.

At the same time, many of the whites I was meeting also did not realize that I was black. While driving me home from a music gig late one night, the older Italian saxophone player who had hired me to play began ranting about the "jungle bunnies" moving into his neighborhood. When I pointed out to him that I was, in fact, a "jungle bunny" myself, he turned beet red. Although he spent the rest of the drive back to my house that night apologizing profusely, an unwritten boundary between us had been crossed. The man never hired me to work with him again.

By the time I was growing up in the 1960s, many of the most overt forms of legal discrimination against African Americans were becoming a thing of the past. It was good to be "black and proud," and it was difficult to imagine why anyone would want to pretend to be white when they weren't. But in J. Ernest's time, anyone with an African American background was guaranteed a lifetime of receiving treatment as a second-class citizen. Black people were routinely barred from many schools, neighborhoods, and professions. In some parts of the country they were denied the right to vote or even to use the same public toilet as a white person. But if one were sufficiently light-skinned, one could avoid the most blatant forms of racial discrimination by pretending to be white. In the black community, this behavior is known as "passing."

Years ago my mother told me that when her aunt Mary Sweeney died in Cincinnati, a number of the "whitest black folks you ever saw" came to the funeral from across the river in Kentucky. Apparently, these people were Sweeneys too, but from "another branch of the family." During the ceremony they kept themselves apart from the other mourners; after the funeral the mysterious relatives crossed back over the Ohio River and into their other lives. Mom assumed these other Sweeneys were "passing" and had stopped by just long enough to pay Aunt Mary their respects. She figured they were related to Aunt Mary somehow, but she felt it best not to ask too many questions. Quite a few African American families have a family member somewhere who is passing for white. It's something that even as a young child you learn not to talk about.

Back in the days when black people were routinely turned down for most jobs, many folks "passed" if they could get away with it so they could get a better job or move into a nicer neighborhood. The problem was that in order to "pass" as white, you had to cut all ties to your life as a black person. Once installed in a new job at a white company or in a new house in a segregated neighborhood, people who passed had to live an inauthentic life, always afraid of being unmasked. Once their true identity was discovered, the folks who were passing would lose any advantages they had gained through this painful masquerade. The decision to "pass" could not be made lightly and, once taken, was difficult to undo.

J. Ernest's eldest son, J. Ernest Jr., was a light-skinned man with hazel eyes. Looking at him, you would never assume that he was black. A brilliant physicist, my Uncle Ernest married Gloria Stewart, a fair-skinned beauty from Chicago's black elite. During the 1950s, 1960s, and 1970s, when many white suburbs were still off-limits to black people, Uncle Ernest lived in a string of then all-white neighborhoods, such as White Plains, New York; La Jolla, California; and Burr Oaks, Illinois.

While never denying his black identity, J. Ernest Jr. didn't exactly shout it from the rooftops either. Visits by Aunt Marjory or any of the darker members of the family were quietly discouraged. Living in those all-white areas, my uncle didn't want to raise any eyebrows or have to answer any unwelcome questions. My mother recalls with a glint in her eye that J. Ernest Jr. "had an apoplectic fit" when a group of his black fraternity brothers gathered on the lawn of his suburban

California home to offer him a housewarming serenade. At the same time, Mom was quick to point out that, because Uncle Ernest did not broadcast his black identity, his children received a free education at a series of excellent suburban schools in nice neighborhoods where blacks would not have been welcomed.[3]

The saddest story I heard about J. Ernest Jr.'s racial ambivalence came from James Montgomery, a fellow Kappa fraternity brother and prominent Chicago attorney. Montgomery is actively involved in the History Keepers, a group that seeks to preserve the stories of African American pioneers. Montgomery had been trying to get Uncle Ernest to participate in the project, to tell his story of what it was like to be one of the first blacks to achieve prominence in physics. But Uncle Ernest refused. He said he wasn't comfortable defining himself as an African American.[4]

Montgomery remembers that when Ernest was teaching at Clark University, a historically black college, many of his students did not believe he was a black man. Only when Ernest told them that he was a Kappa did his students accept him as African American. Montgomery felt Ernest might have been afraid that perhaps, even in the History Keepers, he would not be accepted as black.[5]

Yet, for all that he chose to live in white areas and downplay his African American heritage, Uncle Ernest chose his three wives and his closest friends from the circle of elite African Americans he had known as a child in Chicago. Several years ago, when I asked him about his grandmother Susie Douthit, Uncle Ernest told me he remembered going to visit her in Farmington as a child. When I asked him what Susie looked like, Ernest responded, "Oh, she was a brown-skinned woman." Uncle Ernest then told me that he imagines he would be considered "African American, Negro, whatever you want to call it," too. But Ernest was quick to point out that race is an artificial concept anyway, and we both agreed that maybe someday one's race would no longer carry the importance that it does today.[6]

John Bird Wilkins, my great-grandfather, was a fair-skinned man with wavy hair. As far as I could tell from my research, he always lived in black neighborhoods and was referred to in the press as a "race man," meaning a man who was concerned not just with his own success but with bettering the conditions for the race as a whole. Although he was probably the son of a white man, John Bird lived and died firmly in the bosom of the black community.

My grandfather J. Ernest was also light-skinned. Many newspaper articles written about him made a point of describing him as "a Negro," because, from a photo alone, the reader might not have been able to tell. But J. Ernest lived his whole life as a black man in a rigidly segregated world. He cared deeply about the state of race relations in America and in his own way worked hard to make a difference.

His wife, Lucile, on the other hand seems to have played on both sides of the fence. After receiving her bachelor's degree in mathematics from the University of Chicago in 1923, my grandmother returned to the University of Chicago in 1929 to work on her master's degree. Over the next ten years, between taking care of her husband, teaching full-time in the Chicago public schools, and raising three sons, Lucile continued to take courses and earned a master's degree in education from the University of Chicago in the summer of 1939. When the Colored Methodist Episcopal Church disbanded and joined the previously all-white United Methodist denomination, my grandmother became the first black woman to serve as Women's Division recording secretary for the Methodist Board of Missions.

My mother tells me that Lucile was extremely color conscious and very proud of her fair skin and blue-green eyes. At the fancy all-white resorts where high-level Methodist conferences were held, Lucile was often the only person of color present who was not part of the help. Mom tells me that in these situations my grandmother would not necessarily call attention to her African American racial identity. If people assumed she was white and treated her accordingly, that was just fine with her.[7]

When I interviewed Rocco Siciliano, a friend and colleague of my grandfather's in the Labor Department, about J. Ernest, Siciliano told me a revealing story about how my grandparents handled the issue of race at a dinner party he gave some time in the mid 1950s. Apparently, among Siciliano's dinner guests that evening was a gentleman who used to work for the Herbert Hoover administration. The man's wife, whom Siciliano described as a "stylish, white haired woman," kept making comments about "darkies" every time the black maid who was helping to serve the meal left the room. Concerned that the woman's comments might be making J. Ernest and Lucile uncomfortable, Siciliano began to get "very nervous." But the woman "wanted to be the center of attention or something," so she continued making her racist remarks.

Finally Siciliano told her, "I don't know if you realize it, but the gentleman next to you [J. Ernest] considers himself colored."

Siciliano remembers that the woman challenged him, saying, "I don't believe it. I'm going to ask him."

Siciliano, now really in a panic and afraid the incident would turn ugly, urged her, "Please don't." Siciliano recalls that the woman's "face fell" when she realized that he had been telling the truth. She really had been sitting next to a black man the entire night.

As I listened to Siciliano's story, that old familiar knot in my stomach began to tighten. Being mistaken for white seems to have been our family's curse. For just a moment as Siciliano talked, I was eighteen again, trying to convince a group of white girls that I really was a black person. As Yogi Berra used to say, "déjà vu all over again." But during the 1950s, when people mistook J. Ernest for white, there would have been considerably more at stake.

"What did my grandfather do?" I asked Mr. Siciliano. "Did he challenge the woman or comment about the incident later?"

"No," Siciliano told me. Neither of my grandparents made any comment on the incident to him, either as it was unfolding or later. My grandparents, he said, were "extremely astute in these matters," and perhaps this wasn't the first time they had experienced such an incident. Mr. Siciliano also told me that he knew at the time that Lucile often passed for white, describing her as a "passover." To this day, he says, he remembers how blue her eyes were.

I had never heard this story before, but it did seem to fit the pattern of what I had learned about my grandmother's obsession with skin color. As a child growing up, Lucile had teased and tormented her younger sister, Marjory, for having dark skin. Years later, as Aunt Marj lay dying on her hospital bed, she replayed those horrible scenes from her childhood over and over in her mind, screaming out, "Lucile, I'm black. Please love me! I am not a nigger," over and over, until the nurses came to tranquilize her.

Many African Americans from Aunt Marj's generation were scarred by a deep sense of self-hatred stemming from their skin color. In a world where black skin was despised by the dominant society, having the "proper" skin color was literally a matter of life and death. As the old folks used to say: "If you're white, you're all right. If you're brown, stick around. If you're black, get back."

When Lucile and Aunt Marjory were children, the unequivocal message they received from the dominant society was that being black was a bad thing. Black people were shiftless, ignorant, shuffling morons, fit only for the most menial of positions. Black people were denigrated in popular songs, newspapers, and on the stage. With the advent of cinema, derogatory images of African Americans were soon omnipresent on the silver screen. *Birth of a Nation*, W. B. Griffith's racist paean to the Ku Klux Klan, was the box office smash of 1912. President Woodrow Wilson even held a private screening of the movie in the White House and is supposed to have commented that seeing the film was "like writing history with lightning." Far from questioning the film's blatant racism, Wilson's "only regret" was that its story was "all so terribly true."[8] This color consciousness shaped the world in which J. Ernest rose to prominence. Though light-skinned, he was a black man by birth, breeding, and culture.

As Barack Obama's presidential race picked up steam, the issue of race always lurking under the surface of the American experience took its place at center stage. Everywhere one looked, people were discussing whether this country would be able to consider a black man as a serious presidential candidate. For many on both sides of the racial divide, Obama represented a new kind of black man. Not only was he highly educated and unapologetically articulate, he was equally comfortable around blacks and whites. As the mostly white TV and radio pundits continued to debate the issue, I wondered what my grandfather would have made of all the hubbub. Fifty years ago when J. Ernest walked the halls of power in Washington, he was frequently the only black man not only at the conference table but in the building. What would my grandfather have thought of Obama's candidacy?

After all the hours of research I'd put in, I still had not satisfied my curiosity on the matter of J. Ernest's resignation. I had traced his flamboyant father through three marriages and seventeen children. I had traveled to his birthplace and learned a bit about his strengths and weaknesses as a person. But I still had not found out why my grandfather really left his position at the Labor Department. Other than a few bland profiles from biographical dictionaries, I had little idea of what my grandfather had done or what he had gone through during his five years in Washington. I could almost hear Aunt Marjory's voice whispering in my ear: "You said you were going to preserve the history of the Wilkins family. How can you do that if you don't even know what it is?"

It was time to go back to work. After spending several hours on the Internet, I was able to identify which books about President Eisenhower also mentioned my grandfather. A quick check on WorldCat, a computerized database of library catalogues from around the country, showed me that all of the books I was looking for could be found less than two miles from my house, at Harvard's Widener Library, one of the most visited libraries in the world.

Walking up the wide stone steps to the main building, I passed a group of foreign tourists posing for snapshots. Years ago, one could simply walk into the library, show some ID, and be allowed limited access to their collection. In recent years the growing number of prospective visitors and the increased need for campus security has complicated the procedure for gaining access. After paying a fee, I was photographed and given a visitor's ID card good for no more than six visits within the next year. Once I swiped my new ID card at the security desk, I was escorted up a marble staircase to the Phillips Reading Room for visiting scholars where any material I wished to see would be brought to me. Good thing I already had an idea of the specific books I wanted. There would be no random browsing of the stacks here at Harvard.

Once installed at the comfy oak reading table, I settled in to spend the day. The room was quite large, and a domed skylight flooded the room with natural light. The hush was absolute. Although there were easily thirty people studying in there, you could have heard a pin drop. If I became bored during my research trip, I could always go upstairs and check out the Gutenberg Bible on exhibit under glass in the foyer.

It had taken a fair amount of effort to get myself in here, but I could tell it was going to be worth it. As I waited for my books to be delivered, I checked out the state of the art computers the library had available for in-house reference work. A mega-database of historical newspapers, including all the major black papers from the turn of the last century, was available to Harvard Library users at the click of a mouse. Heaving a quiet sigh of contentment, I began to read.

J. Ernest Wilkins taking the oath of office, 1954

Chapter Thirteen

J. Ernest Wilkins in Washington, 1953–1955

By the early 1950s my grandfather had a reputation in black Chicago as a consummate professional, a "lawyer's lawyer," known for his incisive mind. In the one building in downtown Chicago that would rent to African Americans, a building sarcastically referred to by the city's black attorneys as "Uncle Tom's Cabin," J. Ernest shared office space with some of the city's most influential African Americans, including the future Democratic congressman William L. Dawson.[1] My grandfather was now a member of the United Methodist Church's Judicial Council, the first African American to sit on this prestigious national tribunal. He had received an honorary doctorate from Lincoln University, had served two terms as president of the Cook County Bar Association, and was Grand Polemarch (president) of the Kappa Alpha Psi fraternity.[2]

In 1950 Chicago's Republicans took note of my grandfather's high standing within the community and invited him to run as their candidate for circuit court judge, the first African American to be so honored.[3] William J. Touhy, his opponent in the contest, was supported by Chicago's powerful Democratic machine. Though J. Ernest lost the election, he garnered enough votes to attract the attention of the Republican National Committee.

In an effort to boost their support among black voters, the Republican National Committee members had recently appointed Val Washington as their director of minority affairs. Washington was a member of J. Ernest's fraternity and a longtime Chicago resident. Although it's probable that the two men had already met socially, J. Ernest's rising political star would have given Washington reason to see my grandfather in a new light. When Republican officials began looking for "qualified Negroes" to serve in government after the 1952 election, it's likely that Washington put my grandfather's name at the top of the list. And when President Eisenhower announced that he would be forming a high-level committee to tackle the issue of job discrimination, J. Ernest was chosen to co-chair the group.[4]

To many observers in Washington, D.C., my grandfather's rise to national prominence seemed to come out of the blue. J. Ernest was not really a politician or a civil rights leader. He had not spent any time frequenting the halls of power on Capitol Hill. "Who is this guy? Do you know him?" they would have asked each other, shaking their heads.

Every now and then during my career as a music teacher, I've been lucky enough to watch a student or two rise from obscurity to stardom. One day they're playing for tips in some local dive. Then, before you know it, they're picking up a Grammy on TV. I know that the success that appears to come "overnight" is usually the result of a lot of hard work away from the limelight. When J. Ernest Wilkins was selected to co-chair Eisenhower's first major desegregation initiative, he was nearly sixty years old. He may not have been a household name in Washington, D.C., but my grandfather had been preparing for his moment on the national stage for years.

At the end of the group's first meeting in August 1953, Vice President Richard Nixon announced to reporters that the new committee would be more than a study group. The president, he said, was looking for "concrete action" on discrimination issues. Nixon and my grandfather were the co-chairmen, and the committee's other members included Franklin Delano Roosevelt's son James Roosevelt, the presidents of the American Retail Corporation and International Harvester, and the nation's top two labor leaders, Walter Reuther and George Meany.[5]

Although the White House billed the group as one that would "crack down on discrimination" in firms doing business with the federal government, the committee's mandate was in fact limited. The group would not be empowered legally either to investigate allegations of discrimination or to enforce compliance with its findings. In Eisenhower's words, the committee's main tools would be those of "cooperation, persuasion, education and negotiation."[6] Despite these limitations, the President's Committee on Government Contracts received front-page coverage in the black press and praise from civil rights organizations.[7]

As the only African American on the committee, my grandfather approached his work with a sense of mission. It is the "duty of the church to steer people of high moral standards to run for public office," he told a large crowd at Harlem's St. Mark Methodist Church. Moreover, it is the "right of the people to alter their policy of government when it becomes destructive" to the maintenance of those standards.[8]

The committee's first priority was to address the issue of discrimination in the nation's capital. In meetings chaired alternately by Richard Nixon and by my grandfather, committee members persuaded District of Columbia officials to announce that companies seeking new contracts with the district would be required to show that their hiring practices were not discriminatory. As a result of the committee's efforts, both D.C.'s telephone and bus companies hired black workers for the first time. By November 1953 the committee was able to persuade D.C. commissioners to issue an order banning discrimination in twenty-three city agencies.[9]

However, the committee was not able to achieve all its goals. Bowing to pressure from segregationists in Congress, Washington's fire department was exempted from the new desegregation order. Though the District of Columbia did issue a desegregation order in 1954, it would be years before the fire department truly became an integrated agency.[10]

J. Ernest's work in co-chairing the committee won him Vice President Nixon's respect and also praise from his fellow committee members. In a 1954 editorial, the *New York Times* informed its readers that my grandfather's "qualities of tact, resourcefulness, strength of character and balanced judgment commended themselves to his colleagues."[11] Knowing that the president was considering appointing some African Americans to sub-cabinet positions, Nixon encouraged President Eisenhower to find a place for my grandfather within his administration.[12] In March 1954, J. Ernest received word that he would be appointed to serve as America's first black assistant secretary of labor. Despite the segregated school system in Farmington, Missouri, and despite his impoverished beginnings and his bigamous father, J. Ernest Wilkins would now become the top-ranking African American in the federal government.

I wish I could have been a fly on the wall when he received the news. Just after hanging up the phone, what did my grandfather do? Did he grab Lucile and waltz around the living room? Did he fall down on his knees to shout a prayer of gratitude? Did he pick up the phone and share the news with his three sons? Perhaps my grandfather simply took a moment to savor his triumph in silence. No one still living in my family knows for sure. The one thing we are all positive about is that he did not toast his appointment with a glass of anything alcoholic. J. Ernest did not drink, smoke, swear, or play cards. No matter what else may have been going on in his life, my grandfather would always remain true to the strict Methodist values he had learned as a child in Farmington.

J. Ernest Wilkins's appointment was national news. James Hagerty, Eisenhower's press secretary, announced that it was the "first time, as far as we know, that a Negro has been appointed to a Cabinet or sub-Cabinet post."[13] The statement was not, in fact, strictly accurate. William F. Lewis, an African American, had served as assistant secretary general during the Taft administration.[14] However, no black man had served in a sub-cabinet position in forty years, and never in the Department of Labor.

In a jubilant editorial, the *Chicago Defender* wrote, "Were he alive today, Robert S. Abbott, founder of the *Defender*, . . . might find reason to feel that his many years of arduous campaigning may not have been in vain." The *New York Times* wrote an editorial calling Eisenhower's choice of my grandfather "an excellent appointment." Back in Farmington, reporters chased down J. Ernest's elementary schoolteacher to inquire about her now famous pupil.[15]

At the press conference announcing his nomination, my grandfather told reporters that his appointment "honored his race" more than it honored him as an individual. He reminded his listeners that three-fourths of the world's people were not white. His status as a Negro would, he felt, allow him to work more effectively abroad as a representative of the U.S. government.[16]

Was my grandfather's new position a "token" appointment? There is no question that the White House was looking to increase its popularity with black voters before interim elections took place that November. Speaking to a large black audience in Detroit, Vice President Nixon made sure to let the crowd know that he had "had a hand" in J. Ernest's appointment. He told a reporter from the *Chicago Defender* that the president "had some even bigger jobs planned for Negroes."[17]

By the end of 1954, Eisenhower had appointed ten more blacks to positions within his administration. Eisenhower's eleven African American appointments were the largest number made by any president up to that time. But given the likelihood that Congress would balk at confirming African Americans to high-ranking posts, the appointments were calculated with an eye more to job visibility than to efficacy.[18]

Today, the word "token" is considered pejorative, often used to describe an unqualified person who has been given a job purely on the basis of race. I wish I had a dime for every time I've heard someone tell me, over the last twenty years, that since I am both black and a woman, I must have had an easy time getting my teaching position. "Oh they had to put a black woman in that job," people tell me, implying that without these so-called unfair advantages I would never have qualified. In fact, it's been my experience that "black firsts," far from being less qualified than their white competitors, need to be even more qualified simply to survive on the job. In addition to dealing with the learning curve involved in any new position, African American "firsts" must often be prepared to cope with resentment, suspicion, and outright racist treatment from their white colleagues. As much as we would like to believe that we live in a color-blind society, it's been my experience that the color of your skin has a great deal of influence on the way people treat you.

Back when my grandfather was integrating the Labor Department, things were much worse. The Honorable Anna Diggs Taylor, now a senior U.S. district judge, was fresh out of Yale Law School when my grandfather took her under his wing in June 1957. Despite her Yale law degree, Judge Taylor, an African American, had "no prospects" of finding a job until J. Ernest hired her to work in the Labor Department. "The government was [the world was] VERY openly racist in those days," she explained to me in a letter.[19]

A couple of years ago, over drinks, I asked one of my parents' friends to tell me what it was like for black folks back in the 1950s. With an ironic smile, this accomplished and highly successful black doctor told me the following joke: "What does a white man say to a black redcap? 'Boy, go get my luggage.' What does a white man say to a black bank president? 'Boy, what are you doing in that three-piece suit? Here's a dime. Go get my luggage.'" Though we all laughed heartily, there was no mistaking the bitterness in his tone.

My grandfather's appointment may have been made with an eye to improving the administration's civil rights image. But it was also true that he had done an outstanding job as co-chair of the president's anti-discrimination committee. Standing toe-to-toe with leaders in government, labor, and business, my grandfather with his intelligence, tact, and integrity had won the respect of the second-highest official in the country.

J. Ernest's area of specialization within the Labor Department was to be in the field of international affairs. Barely three months after his appointment J. Ernest, now the head of the U.S. delegation, made his first trip to the International Labor Organization (ILO) convention in Geneva. The *Chicago Defender* has a wonderful photo of my grandfather standing on the tarmac awaiting his flight.[20] He is beaming. The pretty stewardess holding his umbrella for him, and also beaming, is a white girl. One can almost feel the excitement and optimism in the air. This was to be J. Ernest's first appearance on the world stage. If my grandfather was at all nervous, he did not show it.

On the first day of the convention, a veteran delegate from the Middle East approached J. Ernest and asked him how this conference compared with other international conferences he'd attended. In a rare moment of public humor, my grandfather dryly responded, "Well now, that's hard to say. The last international affair I attended on this side of the ocean was in 1918 in France. It was hardly a conference, and any way I was on what you might call the working level, so I really cannot answer your question."[21]

As I read this exchange I laughed out loud, earning startled looks from my fellow scholars in the rarified confines of Harvard's Phillips Reading Room. It was delightful to see this side of my grandfather in print. Everything I had learned about him made him seem so austere. J. Ernest was certainly not a party guy. Nor, as far as I could tell, was he the kind of raconteur who laid folks out with a well-placed joke over dinner. My mother had described him as "cold, stuffy, and pompous," and he was probably all of these things. Yet, at least for this one moment, the record of history had managed to capture a bit of self-deprecating wit. Lovely. I smiled reassuringly at the scholars hunched over their books at my table. After a quick glance over my shoulder to make sure that the head librarian had not phoned security to throw me out, I resumed my reading.

In 1954 the major thrust of American foreign policy involved pursuing a "Cold War" to contain the Soviet Union's growing influence in the world. Communism was considered to be the greatest threat to our nation's security, and many diplomats worried that the emerging nations of Asia and Africa would align with the Soviet Union. When State Department officials tried to contrast the American "Free World" with the dictatorship model put forward by the Communists, many Third World countries scoffed. How could the United States talk about "freedom" and "democracy" when several million of its black citizens were denied even the most basic civil rights? By sending his new, black, assistant secretary of labor to the ILO's Geneva conference, Eisenhower hoped to improve America's image around the world.[22]

As the ILO conference got under way, hostility between the American and the Russian delegations quickly surfaced. Avakimovich Arutyunyan, a Russian delegate with a reputation as a tough debater, declared that Russia was being deprived of its rightful place on the ILO selections committee. The United States, France, and Britain had already gone on record to oppose putting Russia on this important committee. J. Ernest took the podium in response. As he came forward, the reporter covering the event noticed a hush fall over the auditorium.

It seems to me that in the interest of harmony and peace and unity we all should come here not with the idea of saying that ours is the greatest nation in the world, but with the idea of building this organization into the organ for peace it should be. Certainly there are countries here whose boundaries are not so great as others, whose material wealth is not so great, who have not got the natural resources of some, but even they have as great an interest in this body as the greatest of us all. This equality of the ILO should never be forgotten.

After my grandfather finished his speech, the request to add the Russians to the selection committee was defeated by eighty-one votes.[23] The black press crowed at J. Ernest's success. Harold Keith wrote in the *Pittsburgh Courier* that "Most certainly, Mr. Wilkins' statesmanlike conduct before the International Labor Organization in Geneva, when he crossed swords with some of the old heads in the game from behind the so-called 'Iron Curtain' and came out on top, has qualified him to be numbered among our more astute legal minds."[24]

On the last day of the conference, my grandfather gave the keynote address. The United States, he said, is "free and strong" and wants to help the other countries in the world "provide food for the hungry, shelter for the homeless, and strength for the sick." He denounced communist bloc countries for promoting an "empire of slavery to the eastward" whose leaders "use the boot, the gun, and the lie to captivate and oppress. . . . It is easy to be violent, it is easy to hate." The ILO's job, he told the delegates, was "to make peace, to promote life, to seek freedom for all people."[25] My grandfather's first trip to the ILO Convention had been a rousing success—so much so that it inspired Congressman Fred Busbey to have his appropriations committee restore the cuts it had made in J. Ernest's budget.[26]

But my grandfather was given little time to rest on his laurels. In November he was sent to Rome to lead the American delegation at a labor conference there. In this era before cell phones and computers, he wrote my grandmother every day to report on his progress. J. Ernest's letters from this period sparkle with references to state receptions, luncheons with foreign diplomats, and high-level committee meetings. His schedule for the week of November 11 was typical:

6:30PM Monday—Reception by Italian Society
12:30 pm Tuesday—Reception by the Mayor of Rome
9pm Wednesday—Reception by the Minister of Labor of Italy
8:30 PM Thursday—Dinner for the Governing Body
6:30 Friday—Reception by the Minister of Foreign affairs.

Later in the same letter, he tells my grandmother that "the date and hour of our visit to the Vatican has not been set."[27]

My grandfather's daily letters home, often little more than lists of times and dates, reveal a man who was proper, correct, and restrained even in his most private communications. Although he was not a man to show his emotions publicly, I suspect that the attention, recognition, and accolades J. Ernest received for his work abroad meant a lot to him. He was being feted on a regular basis by ambassadors and high-ranking government officials. It must have been heady stuff for the son of a laundress from Farmington, Missouri.

The environment back in Washington, however, was considerably less welcoming. Although administration officials were happy to display an African American to the world as an antidote to communist propaganda, many White House staffers were reluctant to accept a black man as their professional equal. E. Frederick Morrow, Eisenhower's administrative assistant, was the first black man ever hired to work in an executive capacity at the White House. He described the attitude of many White House staffers as "condescending to blacks generally."[28] For example, Jack Anderson, later to become a noted Washington columnist, casually used the word "nigger" when telling a joke in Morrow's presence at a staff meeting. When Morrow asked him to repeat himself, Anderson looked him dead in the eye and repeated the slur without apology.[29]

When Morrow first began working at the White House, many of the white women in the secretarial pool refused to work for him. Feeling himself "under scrutiny" at all times, Morrow found it necessary to meet with his female staff in groups "to avoid any damaging gossip."[30] From the beginning, Morrow felt himself "shut out" from serious policy discussions by other White House staffers, and he later wrote of the "paternalistic attitude" many Republican leaders had toward blacks.[31]

As the Labor Department's lone black official, my grandfather would no doubt have received similar treatment. But unlike Morrow, J. Ernest was an intensely private man. If he was refused service in a D.C. restaurant, he simply held his anger inside. And though he was an avid golfer, my grandfather never publicly protested the fact that blacks were not allowed to use the links at Burning Tree, the president's favorite country club. After leaving the White House, Morrow wrote a book about his encounters with racism there. J. Ernest never publicly complained. If someone made rude or racist comments in his presence, although he may have been inwardly livid, my grandfather kept his thoughts to himself.

The more I thought about the stoicism with which J. Ernest faced the adversities in his life, the more I thought about my father. Back in the 1970s, Dad was the first black man in Chicago to become a partner in a large white law firm. Although much ado was made about this at the time, truth was, Dad was miserably unhappy at his new job. For over a year, he held his frustrations inside and soldiered on, going regularly off to work and sharing his feelings with no one. Then one Saturday morning, he threw a bunch of boxes in the back of the family station wagon, packed up his law books, and moved out of his office. Presumably he had informed his fellow partners before he left the firm, but at home Dad had kept his intentions to himself. His silence through what must have been months of miserable agony on the job hurt my mother deeply and mystified the rest of us. But now, reading about J. Ernest, I began to see how my Dad had acquired his penchant for secrecy.

J. Ernest Wilkins had never been a quitter or a whiner. Not in Farmington when kids teased him about his absent father. Not at the University of Illinois when he had to work long hours after school in order to support himself. Not in the army where he faced death and vicious racial prejudice on a daily basis. Rather than make a fuss, my grandfather simply redoubled his efforts to show the world that a black man could excel at whatever task was put before him.

On August 16, 1954, J. Ernest Wilkins again made history when he became the first black man to participate in a cabinet meeting. The fact that his cabinet appearance may have been arranged as part of a calculated publicity stunt by the administration does not take away from the fact that he was indeed there, the first black man ever to sit around the big oval table with the president and his highest-ranking officers.[32] During the meeting, all the cabinet officials welcomed J. Ernest cordially, while Vice President Nixon made it a point to elicit my grandfather's views on international affairs. As he was leaving the meeting, reporters asked how he had felt about being part of such a historic occasion. I am proud of J. Ernest's response. If the reporters had expected my grandfather to shuffle and grin with gratitude for this opportunity to sit down at the White Man's Table, they would have been sorely disappointed. "Of course, this was an unusual experience," he responded, "but I have attended a great many meetings, and I tried to regard this as just another meeting."[33]

In May of 1954 the Supreme Court issued its now famous *Brown v. Board of Education of Topeka* decision, overthrowing the legal basis for segregated schools. If I had to choose one piece of legal history that has made the most difference for me personally, I would have to put the *Brown* decision at the top of the list. I was barely two when the nation's schools were desegregated, but the *Brown* decision opened doors of opportunity that previously would never have been available to me. Like many black folks, J. Ernest was optimistic about the state of American race relations in light of the *Brown* decision. "The members of the Supreme Court by their unanimous history-making decision in May decided this case as Americans, as men dedicated to the preservation of the nation that was founded on the principles of the Constitution," he told an elite group of black professionals in Philadelphia.[34]

Over the next three years, J. Ernest's duties as the Labor Department's international affairs representative kept him traveling constantly. In November 1954 he was sent to Rome, and in the spring and summer of 1955, to Geneva. In the summer of 1956, he once again led the American delegation at the ILO Convention, where two Hungarian delegates were refused participation in the convention to protest the Russian takeover of that nation's government.[35]

As one of a tiny handful of high-profile African American Republicans, my grandfather's presence was in constant demand as the 1956 presidential election heated up. In the fall of 1956, J. Ernest represented the United States at a labor conference in Cuba and then rushed back to Tucson to give a speech in support of the Eisenhower ticket before Election Day. Meanwhile, he had been asked to be part of yet another committee investigating bias in procedures used to award government contracts. Convened in January 1955, the President's Committee on Government Employment Practices was charged with ascertaining the status of blacks employed by the government and increasing the number of African Americans in high-level positions.

But from the beginning the committee encountered severe obstacles. Few black employees were willing to risk their jobs by coming forward to make a complaint. The information-gathering process was hampered by the fact that employees who did wish to lodge a complaint were required to travel great distances, at their own expense, to attend the committee's hearings. And the procedural deck was stacked against those still wishing to make a formal complaint.

The committee's hearing process mandated that the full burden of proof rested on the complainant, not on the government agency accused of discrimination. At the same time, the committee's procedures routinely denied complainants access to the government files they needed to prepare their cases, claiming that the files contained "sensitive information." It is not at all surprising that few complaints were filed under this Kafkaesque system.[36]

Despite the failure of the new contract committee to make many changes in government hiring practices, J. Ernest continued to advocate equal employment whenever he could. At his insistence, two African American staffers were included in the American delegation at the 1957 ILO convention.[37]

As 1956 came to a close, J. Ernest Wilkins appeared to have won the respect of colleagues both at home and abroad. At the Republican National Convention, J. Ernest gave a speech to second Richard Nixon's vice-presidential nomination. In that proud moment it must have seemed that all his struggle and hard work had paid off. As he often told reporters, times were changing for the better and discrimination was "fast fading from the American scene."[38] When the distinguished South African writer and anti-apartheid activist Alan Paton came to Washington to investigate the state of American race relations in the wake of the *Brown v. Board of Education* decision, one of the first people he interviewed was J. Ernest Wilkins. When asked about the future of the Negro in America, my grandfather replied, "It is full of hope. It has never been so full of hope."[39]

But my grandfather was wrong. Behind the public façade of accolades and glamorous parties, the political culture in Washington would remain tainted by unremitting racism. Within the next year, J. Ernest Wilkins would begin to doubt his earlier optimism.

ILO Delegation (left to right): Burger, Kammholz, Langlie, Wilkins

Chapter Fourteen

In Washington, 1955–1957

After months of painstaking research I was on the verge of finding out what had caused my grandfather to leave the Labor Department. I had pestered my older relatives and friends of the family for information. I had spent hours in libraries and hundreds of dollars on books. I had worn out my researcher, Mariah Cooper, with scores of questions. I had flown more than a thousand miles to see the place where J. Ernest's story began. I had checked and double-checked information drawn from old newspapers, census data, and tax rolls.

I was almost at the end of my search. There was only one small problem. I was driving my husband crazy.

When a two-foot-high stack of books on the Eisenhower era crashed to the floor during one of my late-night research sessions, John, startled awake by the noise, confronted me.

"Carolyn, what on earth are you doing? It's nearly two a.m." He rubbed his eyes and peered at me accusingly.

"I'm sorry, honey. I didn't mean to wake you. I was looking for this great quote I found about J. Ernest. I know the book is here somewhere—I was just looking at it a minute ago. It's by Robert Burk. It's got a gray cover. You've got fresh eyes. Could you just take a look around? Maybe you can find it. I just had it not five minutes ago." Focused on my task, I continued to dig through the pile of books at my feet.

My husband took me by the shoulders and turned me toward him, the chill in his voice commanding my full attention.

"Carolyn. You know I have to get up early in the morning. You wake me out of a sound sleep and don't even apologize? Then you have the nerve to ask me to look for a *book?*"

Well, it was not just any old book. It was *the* book that might contain vital clues about J. Ernest's time in D.C. But, of course, John was right. I might have been acting just a tiny bit obsessive.

"I'm sorry, honey. It's just that I'm so close to figuring out why J. Ernest quit his Labor gig. That's the whole reason I started this search. The answer's right here. I can feel it."

"Carolyn, this thing has gotten completely out of hand." John's bleary eyes, now fully focused, glanced angrily around my cramped study. "Look at this place. You spend hours in here each day. You don't go out, you barely play your music anymore. I can't remember when we've spent a quiet evening at home just hanging out. I love you and I know your grandfather is important to you, but I *cannot* go on like this indefinitely."

"Of course, of course, baby, I know. I can't go on forever like this either." When I looked at my behavior from John's perspective, the sight was not pretty.

"You are totally right about everything, John. I know I've been distracted and difficult. This thing about my grandfather has been tearing me up inside. Every day I wake up with this ridiculous hunger to find out what really happened to him. I know it's crazy. I *know*. And you are beyond a saint to put up with me like this. And I'm really, really, *really* sorry I woke you up. It won't happen again, I promise."

My husband stood stiffly among the books and papers scattered on the floor and allowed me to give him a hug.

"OK Carolyn. Here's what we'll do. While you are on vacation from school, do your thing. Spend twenty-four hours a day in your study if you want. But come September, I want my wife back. I know your research is important to you, but it's been three years. Enough is enough."

John was right. It was time to rein myself in. I had taxed the limits of my marriage, the patience of my family, and the boundaries of my sanity. But I was so close to finding out why my grandfather had resigned from the Labor Department.

"Alright, love. You got a deal. I will work like crazy for the next few weeks, and come September, no later than the end of September, I will be done. How does that sound?"

John smiled. "Carolyn, you really are a lawyer's daughter. I say September, and somehow you've managed to extend it until the end of the month. Pretty tricky negotiating. But OK. September 30. And that's it. I get my wife back, no ifs, ands, or buts. Do we have a deal?"

My knees sagged with relief. I love my husband to death and really cannot function if he's angry with me. John's deadline would be tough to meet, but come hell or high water I would do it.

"Deal." I shook his hand formally and gave him a peck on the cheek to seal the bargain.

"Alright, Carolyn. I'm going to hold you to it. And clean up this room. Each day it's a worse mess than the day before. You'll never get any quality work done in this sty."

The next day when I came home from grocery shopping, I found a brand-new bookcase leaning against the door to my study. Stuck to the case was a giant yellow PostIt. "Getting organized is half the battle," it read. "Happy early (or late) Valentine's Day. I love you—John."

Believe me, I know just exactly how lucky I am.

The next day I drove out to Fitchburg State College. Fitchburg is a Massachusetts state school with only a fraction of Harvard's endowment. But it was Fitchburg's library, not Harvard's, that contained the information I now needed to continue my research. My grandfather's resignation had been covered extensively in the black press, and I was hoping to find an in-depth piece that *Ebony* magazine had written about him. The library at Fitchburg State College was the one place within a five-hundred-mile radius where I could read old copies of *Ebony* on microfilm.

Fitchburg's enrollment, like that of most colleges, is smaller for the summer term. As I took my place by the microfilm reader, the librarian and I were the only people in the room. I threaded the microfilm through its spool and adjusted the focus. Outside, it was a hot July day but inside the library's large, modern reading room, the air felt crisp and inviting. As I settled into my task, the sounds, sights, and smells of the outside world fell away. I was no longer Carolyn Wilkins, a twenty-first-century academic trying to discover her grandfather's past. For the next few hours the pages of *Ebony* magazine would place me at the center of one of most turbulent times in the history of American race relations.

On August 27, 1955, Emmett Till, a fourteen-year-old African American boy from Chicago, was visiting relatives in Mississippi. The night after Carolyn Bryant, a clerk at the local general store, accused Till of whistling at her, the boy was taken from his uncle's home at gunpoint, tortured for several hours, and finally killed by Bryant's husband and a brutal gang of whites. When Till's mutilated body was recovered from the Tallahassee River several days later, his mother, in a terrifying act of courage, refused to have the body restored in any way by the undertaker. At the funeral in Chicago, thousands of people kept vigil outside a South Side church where shocked and grieving mourners filed respectfully past the boy's open casket. The pictures of Emmett Till's battered and broken body appeared in newspapers around the world and seared the minds of a generation of black Americans.[1]

In a cramped and steamy Mississippi courtroom several weeks later, an all-white jury found Bryant's husband and brother-in-law not guilty of murder, despite eyewitness testimony linking them to the crime. In that terrible moment, the modern civil rights movement took a new leap forward. From speakers' platforms across the country, black and white politicians denounced the verdict. Meanwhile, white violence against blacks across the South intensified.

As white school districts across the country prepared to open their doors to black students, in compliance with the *Brown* decision, blacks and whites alike feared even greater racial violence.[2]

On December 19, 1955, Max Rabb, Eisenhower's unofficial expert on "minority affairs," called a meeting with my grandfather, Morrow, and five other high-ranking black Republicans to discuss civil rights issues. "We were unanimous," Morrow later recalled, "in feeling that the White House should have spoken out on the Till case." Rabb responded that he was "under pressure from various factions" within the administration because of his civil rights advocacy. As Morrow put it, "some members of the staff, as well as the Cabinet, are utterly conservative on the matter of race."[3]

Despite the administration's refusal to make any kind of moral statement to the nation about the murder of Emmett Till, Rabb expected that Eisenhower's black appointees would campaign vigorously for the president in the upcoming election. In the presidential election of 1952, Eisenhower had received less than 30 percent of the black vote.[4] Republican officials were especially concerned with the results of a recent Gallup poll indicating that the majority of African Americans still favored the Democratic Party. Administration official Howard Pyle, who, though not invited to the meeting, had attended anyway, was critical of black voters. Eisenhower had "bent over backwards" on the issue of civil rights, he said. In continuing to support the Democrats, black voters had not shown any "gratitude" for his efforts. He told my grandfather and the other black men gathered in the room that they needed to "get out into the field and preach loyalty" to the black community.[5]

My guess is that the black Republicans gathered in the room that day resented the inference that they had not been hard at work supporting the party's programs. As the 1956 election campaign got under way, my grandfather was part of an elite corps of black public speakers charged with bringing Eisenhower's message to the black community. "With the President planning to confine his campaign to a few major speeches and television programs," columnist Levi Jolley noted in the *Pittsburgh Courier,* "you can expect a complete new approach with many present appointees going from town to town drumming up the votes."[6]

In February 1956, J. Ernest addressed the Urban League banquet in New York City. In April, he flew from Washington to participate in a star-studded fund-raiser featuring hotel magnate Conrad Hilton, Vice President Richard Nixon, and Illinois senator Everett Dirksen. In May my grandfather was on the stump again, this time addressing the party faithful in Minnesota.

While my grandfather traveled the country speaking on behalf of the administration's civil rights policies, the country's racial climate continued to worsen, however. Scholar Robert Burk notes that the fall semester of 1955 witnessed only minimal progress toward desegregating southern schools. No desegregation whatever was reported in Georgia, Mississippi, Louisiana, Alabama, Florida, North Carolina, South Carolina, Tennessee, or Virginia. In Hoxie, Arkansas, massive protests and a lawsuit by the local White Citizens' Council forced the local school board to close their schools down rather than desegregate.[7]

In December 1955, Morrow sent a memo to the president's chief of staff asking that the president take a more visible stand on civil rights. The flamboyant African American congressman Adam Clayton Powell had proposed an amendment to a school construction bill that would deny federal funding for segregated schools. But the administration, stressing the pressing need for new classrooms, was not interested in supporting an amendment that was likely to antagonize influential southern legislators. When Powell offered to withdraw his proposal if the White House would pledge to enforce the Supreme Court's decision to integrate the nation's schools, the president disowned any executive responsibility for implementing the desegregation order.[8]

Meanwhile, southern resistance to desegregation continued to intensify. When a black woman named Autherine Lucy attempted to enroll at the University of Alabama, she was stoned by an angry mob of whites. When Lucy sued the university for failing to protect her from mob violence, she was expelled from the school. On orders from administration officials, the Justice Department took no action in Lucy's case, refusing to intervene in what was considered a matter of "state's rights."[9]

Undeterred, civil rights activists continued to push for desegregation. In December 1955, blacks led by the Reverend Dr. Martin Luther King began a yearlong boycott of the segregated bus system in Montgomery, Alabama. Once again, the Eisenhower administration was given an opportunity to demonstrate moral leadership in support of integration initiatives when Dr. King was thrown in jail by city authorities. On February 24, 1956, Adam Clayton Powell sent an urgent telegram asking the president to intervene on King's behalf. But Eisenhower showed little inclination to get involved in what he saw as a local matter. "As I understand it, there is a state law about boycotts, and it is under that kind of thing that these people are being brought to trial," he stated.[10]

As my grandfather shuttled about the country making campaign appearances on behalf of the president, and as he attempted to defend U.S. policies to foreign critics at labor conferences abroad, J. Ernest must have felt some frustration with the administration's hands-off stance toward federal enforcement of the *Brown* decision. His colleague E. Frederick Morrow noted passionately in his diary the deep conflict he often felt in having to defend the administration's policies to critical black audiences. "I am more and more conscious of the great personal problem . . . of being two personalities at once—a Negro and an American," Morrow wrote.[11]

Unlike Morrow, my grandfather never commented publicly on the Montgomery bus boycott or the activities of Dr. Martin Luther King. My guess is that as a "lawyer's lawyer," J. Ernest would have preferred to lobby for civil rights in the courtroom rather than demonstrate in ways that provoked the local authorities. But as one southern school district after another openly defied the *Brown* decision, it must have pained my grandfather that his president refused to take a more active role in enforcing the law of the land. But Eisenhower remained determined to stay out of the desegregation controversy. "Another system was upheld by the Supreme Court for sixty years" before the *Brown* decision, the president told Attorney General Brownell in a confidential memo. "Ever since the 'separate but equal' decision, they [the South] have been obeying the Constitution of the United States."[12] J. Ernest had lived through the injustices of the so-called separate but equal system. If he had seen this memo, I wonder if he would have worked so hard on the president's reelection campaign.

My grandfather was not a political man. He had attained his position because of intellectual brilliance, not because of any ability to be a team player. A staunch Methodist who didn't drink, smoke, or swear, J. Ernest had a deeply ingrained sense of right and wrong, and once he had decided on a position he could be inflexible.[13] As the racial climate in the country worsened, my grandfather did begin to show public dissatisfaction with the jobs being made available for African Americans.

In a speech before the National Urban League in February 1956, J. Ernest summed up his thoughts on the current state of employment opportunities for blacks: "It is like the remark that was made at a recent dinner party in Washington. A lady is reported to have said, 'I tried to get a white maid, but they wanted so much money. I finally had to hire a colored girl. You know, it makes us feel so broad-minded.' As I said, though the economic position of Negroes is improving, their competitive position has not improved to the same degree."[14]

Later that spring, J. Ernest told an audience of black postal workers that much more work needed to be done in the area of creating equal employment opportunities for African Americans. "What we are after is not a few jobs in the foundry, a little token employment in the accounting department. We want effective protection from the top of industry for the qualified Negro competitor for any job which industry has to offer."[15] I can imagine that the strain of being a public spokesman for an administration that had failed to deliver on the promises of the *Brown* decision was beginning to tell on my grandfather. Back in Washington, his relationship with his boss was also beginning to sour.

James P. Mitchell had been the head of the Labor Department for only a few months before my grandfather began his duties there. Although both men were roughly the same age, they came from vastly different worlds. The son of working-class Catholics in Elizabeth, New Jersey, Mitchell had worked

his way up through the ranks of government service, serving as a county su-
pervisor, in the WPA, and in the labor relations division of the army construction program. During the war he had been the director of industrial personnel
for the War Department before taking a civilian job as the head of personnel
for Bloomingdale's department store empire. Eisenhower had known Mitchell
from his work in the army, and when his first secretary of labor resigned after
serving only ten months in the job, Eisenhower appointed Mitchell to head
the department.[16]

Widely respected as an administrator, Mitchell was a stickler for detail and
was well-known for being tough on his staff. According to Rocco Siciliano, who
also served as an assistant secretary of labor during this period, Mitchell was
proud of the fact that he had worked his way up through the ranks without
benefit of a college education. In fact, Siciliano states that during staff meetings
Mitchell would delight in reminding his more educated subordinates of this
fact.[17]

My grandfather had not exactly been born with a silver spoon in his mouth
either, of course. But there was no way J. Ernest would even have been hired
by the Labor Department without a college degree. A black man needed all
the credentials he could muster simply to be placed in the running for a high-
level position. During the 1950s many college-educated blacks had to take jobs
in factories and post offices because white employers refused to hire African
Americans in leadership roles, no matter how well-educated they were.

Like Secretary Mitchell, J. Ernest Wilkins was a hard worker with a passion
for detail. But as a "Negro first," my grandfather was forced to step into a demanding high-profile job without the benefit of a mentor or any previous experience of working in Washington's bureaucratic jungle. Hired on the basis
of his work with the President's Committee on Government Contracts rather
than because of any connections within the world of labor, my grandfather
was a fish out of water among the former union men with whom he worked.
Since many labor unions at this time were strictly segregated by race, several of
the men with whom J. Ernest interacted on a daily basis were not comfortable
working with a black man as their professional equal.[18]

As a man who came from a very traditional culture where elders were respected and never publicly contradicted, my grandfather would have found his
new work environment disconcerting, to say the least. In 1956 my grandfather
was already sixty-two years old. James Mitchell was ten years his junior, while
the thirty-five-year-old Siciliano was at the same level as J. Ernest in the Labor
Department hierarchy.

Mitchell could be charming to outsiders. But he was "a very tough, driving taskmaster" who could be abrupt, even inconsiderate, with members of
his own staff.[19] J. Ernest had a great deal of pride in his educated status and in

that of his family. For a man of my grandfather's background, to be addressed bluntly, perhaps inconsiderately, in front of others by someone who was not even a college graduate would have been deeply humiliating. It would have really rankled, I expect, though I doubt J. Ernest would have let his annoyance show.

Within three months of starting to work at the Labor Department, my grandfather had been chosen to head the American delegation to a major international conference. He had given major speeches on government policy. He had seen his opinions solicited by the vice president in a cabinet meeting. I am sure, by 1956, my grandfather would have felt he was handling his job pretty well. But, lacking the mentoring support that is available to most people when they step into a new leadership position, J. Ernest was unable to interpret the hints and early warning signs of the labor secretary's dissatisfaction.

In April 1955, my grandfather was asked to prepare a monthly report on labor developments around the world. Then, through his assistant John Gilhooley, Mitchell expressed dissatisfaction with the report J. Ernest had written. Gilhooley sent the report back down the chain of command and asked his assistant Millard Cass to speak to my grandfather about changing it. "Material referred to is a sheaf of twenty-five pages reciting picayune details of labor developments in various countries," Gilhooley explained to Cass in a memo. "What the boss wants is a monthly report on major and significant developments through the world in the broadest strokes and confined to a couple of pages—readable prose." Then, using a tactic familiar to administrators the world over, Gilhooley told Cass, "I would appreciate your doing what you can to give Wilkins an idea of how he ought to go about this without indicating that this request was made to you."[20]

Perhaps Gilhooley was trying to spare J. Ernest's feelings or avoid a direct confrontation. Whatever he was trying to do, however, Cass's "hints" to my grandfather failed to yield the desired result. Cass sent back his own memo: "Wilkins says not feasible to make brief of this—he believes the Secretary merely wants to see how this information is compiled." A week later Gilhooley returned J. Ernest's report again, stating, "I am returning this to you in accordance with my memorandum to you of Abril 6th. The secretary would like these monthly reports to commence May 1st." But J. Ernest apparently held firm. On yet another Gilhooley memo, Mitchell scrawls an exasperated note at the bottom of the page: "Jack—The same type matter again!"[21]

My grandfather was nothing if not stubborn. It was stubbornness that had gotten him through all the difficult times in his life, and it seems he wasn't going to change now. J. Ernest was a novice in the complex world of government bureaucracy. Before he joined the Labor Department, he had always been his own boss. If there was a problem with something he did, J. Ernest would take his case straight to the man at the top. And if my grandfather felt he was really right about something, no matter what the boss said, he would stick to his position.

J. Ernest's early memos and reports on his activities in the ILO indicate he was not afraid to take on other departments or agencies that he felt were impinging on his turf. Unskilled at the art of political infighting, my grandfather probably stepped on the toes of several officials when he wrote Mitchell that "Practically everything we do requires the concurrence of the Department of State—which is not always forthcoming. Conversely, State often acts unilaterally on matters of direct interest to the Department of Labor." In this 1956 annual report, my grandfather states that "lack of policy and overall program formulation in the labor field in Washington" has hampered his department's efforts abroad. In point after point, he criticizes the "negative attitude" of U.S. employers toward the ILO and the unwillingness of the U.S. government to support popular ILO agenda items such as sanctions against the use of forced labor. Time and again, J. Ernest presses his bosses for additional funding and more staff.[22]

At the close of the 1956 ILO conference, Mitchell shoots J. Ernest an ironic note: "Wouldn't it be a good idea to request each member of this year's Government Delegation to ILO to give you 1. An *honest* critique on the conference. 2. Suggestions for improving our position in ILO."[23] It's only a short memo, but it seems to indicate some dissatisfaction with the way things went at the conference.

In an article written three years later, Simeon Booker quotes an anonymous labor official as saying that J. Ernest was "too honest, too sincere to realize his role as a diplomat." During the 1957 ILO conference, for example, a Russian delegate took the floor and gave a rousing speech attacking racial injustices in the United States. Other members of the U.S. delegation wanted J. Ernest to silence the delegate, but my grandfather refused to do so, saying, "He's telling the truth, isn't he."[24]

By 1957 Secretary Mitchell had become increasingly displeased with J. Ernest's work and was looking for a way to remove him from his position as assistant secretary.[25] Perhaps my grandfather was aware of his boss's dissatisfaction with his performance. If so, he kept it to himself. In *Ebony* magazine, Booker described J. Ernest as a man who "took little advice, had few friends in labor areas and worked almost independently." Booker quotes one black labor leader as saying that my grandfather "never picked up the phone or dropped by."[26] My grandfather's tendency toward self-reliance and stoicism had gotten him far in life, but as the year 1957 came to a close, these same personality traits were beginning to work against him.

On the national stage, relationships between blacks and whites in the South had reached a crisis point. Southern cities resisted attempts to integrate their school districts in accordance with the *Brown v. Board* decision. In the fall of 1957, the Little Rock school board ordered Central High School to begin admitting black students. Arkansas governor Orville Faubus, an astute politician who avidly courted segregationist voters, was determined to defy the U.S. Supreme Court's desegregation decision. As the first day of the 1957 school term approached, Governor Faubus called out the Alabama National Guard, not to protect the nine black students who would be attending Central High but to keep them off school property. On the first day of school the situation in Little Rock spiraled rapidly out of control. Jeering mobs of white segregationists chased and beat the black students who were attempting to enter the school, as soldiers from the Alabama National Guard stood idly by. In the months leading up to the Little Rock confrontation, advocates within the administration had attempted to get the president to take a greater leadership role in the school desegregation controversy. But Eisenhower continued to reject all suggestions for a White House conference on desegregation.[27]

"If you go too far too fast," on the issue of school desegregation, the president told his attorney general, "you are making a mistake."[28]

"It is difficult," a frustrated E. Frederick Morrow confided to his diary, "for me to explain to my friends why the President will not . . . admonish the South on its outright flouting of *Brown*."[29]

My grandfather was a vigorous supporter of school desegregation. He told an audience in 1954 that those who opposed the *Brown* decision were "opposing the whole concept of law and order, the whole concept of human rights on which their security is founded." In that same speech, my grandfather praised the NAACP for their hard work during the long series of court battles that led to the Supreme Court's groundbreaking decision in the *Brown* case.[30] But as the Little Rock crisis unfolded, I could find no evidence that J. Ernest Wilkins commented publicly on the situation. It is likely that my grandfather, like his black colleague E. Frederick Morrow, was "powerless to do anything" and was "too well-schooled in protocol" to offer unsolicited advice to the president."[31]

President Eisenhower was indeed caught between a rock and a hard place. On the one hand, his whole philosophy of government revolved around respect for states' rights and local traditions. On the other hand, *Brown v. Board* was now the official law of the land. As the country's commander in chief, it was Eisenhower's sworn duty to enforce desegregation whether he personally agreed with it or not.

As the situation in Little Rock worsened, the president vacillated, hoping to negotiate a compromise with Governor Faubus. But after three weeks of mob violence in Little Rock, the president had had enough. On September 24, 1957, Eisenhower ordered troops from the 101st Airborne Division into the city to enforce the law and restore public order. The story was custom made for the brand-new medium of television, which carried into living rooms around the world the image of armed U.S. troops escorting the nine black children up the steps of Central High.

Civil rights leaders were quick to express support for the president's actions. Dr. Martin Luther King cabled President Eisenhower: "The overwhelming majority of southerners, Negro and white, stand firmly behind your resolute action." The parents of the nine black students involved in the crisis wrote a grateful letter to the president to let him know that his actions had strengthened their faith in democracy.[32]

In the wake of the Little Rock crisis, Eisenhower officials decided to revive a civil rights bill that the attorney general had tried to push through Congress the year before. Despite the active opposition of many conservatives and despite a twenty-four-hour filibuster by South Carolina senator Strom Thurmond, a compromise bill was passed and signed into law in November. Among other provisions, the Civil Rights Act of 1957 required that a bipartisan commission be established to investigate allegations of discrimination across the country. Eisenhower's hope was that the commission would have an "ameliorating effect" on the passions aroused by the school desegregation crisis.[33] To serve on the new commission, the president hoped to find "thoughtful men" who would represent the "full spectrum" of opinion on civil rights.[34] To this end, the commissioners would represent the North and the South in equal numbers. One spot on the Civil Rights Commission would be reserved for an African American.[35]

In October 1957, Eisenhower's Chief of Staff Sherman Adams met with E. Frederick Morrow. Adams wanted Morrow's confidential opinion on my grandfather's suitability for the job. Morrow wrote about the conversation, "I told him that I felt that Secretary of Labor Wilkins was well qualified, that the Senate would confirm him without difficulty, and that he was esteemed by both Negro and white citizens. He is an able man and could bring objective thinking to this difficult problem." When Adams asked if he had any other recommendations for the commission in the event J. Ernest should turn down the job, Morrow was hard-pressed to think of anyone else who would be suitable. "While there are scores of highly educated widely respected Negroes in this country, the character of this commission demands an exceptional Negro member," he wrote in his diary after the meeting. "I am hoping that Ernest Wilkins will not turn down the request."[36]

For entirely different reasons, Labor Secretary Mitchell had similar hopes. Perhaps, if my grandfather had a position on the Civil Rights Commission, he would be willing to resign from the Labor Department. In a not-too-subtle letter, Mitchell forwards to J. Ernest a copy of a speech on civil rights by New York congressman Kenneth Keating. "I heard Congressman Keating make this very fine speech and I would like to call your attention particularly to his comments on the functions and opportunities of the Civil Rights Commission," Mitchell wrote.[37]

In the end my grandfather accepted the president's invitation to join America's first Civil Rights Commission. It was a historic moment for a poor boy from Farmington, Missouri. Standing in front of the president with the rest of the commission members in November 1957, my grandfather looks solemn but proud as he takes the oath of office.[38]

Much to Secretary Mitchell's disappointment, however, my grandfather refused to resign his position at the Labor Department. Throughout the fall of 1957 and the spring of 1958, J. Ernest continued to churn out reports, letters, and memos in preparation for the annual ILO spring meeting in Geneva.[39] My grandfather was particularly excited about a position paper on job discrimination that he wanted the U.S. delegation to present at the Geneva conference. On April 25, 1958, he forwarded a copy of it to Secretary Mitchell. In this paper J. Ernest refers both to the *Brown* decision and to the President's Committee on Governmental Contracts.

It is not possible to separate discrimination in employment and occupation from discrimination in other fields. For example, on May 17, 1954, the U.S. Supreme Court in a unanimous decision declared that segregation in public education imposed by State law is a denial of the equal protection of the laws guaranteed in the 14th Amendment. Admission to public vocational training and vocational schools in the United States is currently guided by this decision.[40]

Although J. Ernest's language seems bland enough today, the southern congressmen who held the department's purse strings viewed any official statement supporting school desegregation as anathema. The State Department had already expressed concerns over the position paper. In April and early May, my grandfather held a series of meetings with State Department officials to discuss his position paper.[41]

On May 9, 1958, J. Ernest forwarded the list of people he wanted added to his delegation at the ILO up the chain of command.[42] As the convention's date approached, my grandfather cleared his calendar and made final preparations for the trip to Geneva. But shortly before his planned departure, J. Ernest was told he would not be making the trip with the rest of his delegation.[43]

Although the warning signs had been clear for some time, I honestly believe my grandfather did not see the blow coming. As Booker reported in *Ebony*, J. Ernest Wilkins was "a man dedicated to what he believed was right." Once he had made up his mind, he would not stray from his course of action.[44] But now it was too late. It seems that Secretary Mitchell, a veteran bureaucrat, was determined to force J. Ernest's resignation from the Labor Department.

My grandfather must have been devastated. Preparing for and attending the ILO convention had been the major focus of his professional life in government. Three days after the U.S. delegation left for Geneva without him, my grandfather suffered a heart attack while at work and was rushed to Walter Reed Hospital, and this is where he spent the next three months. The illness was nearly fatal, and for several weeks doctors worried that he would be permanently blinded. Even in the midst of this severe personal and professional crisis, however, J. Ernest refused to reach out for help. Booker reports one Negro Republican as saying, "If we'd just known what was going on, we could have helped. But Wilkins was a self-reliant man."[45]

He was also a proud and deeply self-critical man. I believe my grandfather's failure to win the esteem of his superiors at the Labor Department wounded him profoundly. All his life J. Ernest had driven himself to be the top achiever in any and all endeavors. The sarcastic criticism he meted out to his sons for even the smallest of mistakes would have been nothing compared to the way he punished himself for in any way not excelling on the job. Failure at any level would have been deeply shameful and totally unacceptable to him.

I believe he was incapable of sharing his pain with anyone. J. Ernest had survived the many traumatic events in his life by not allowing himself to be overwhelmed by emotions. He had made a success of himself despite the odds. He had not given up as a boy in Farmington, Missouri. He had not given up as a young man in the army. And, although his situation appeared hopeless, J. Ernest Wilkins would not give up now.

When my grandfather returned to work in July 1958, he found he had been stripped of almost all his former job responsibilities and was without even a full-time secretary. Booker describes J. Ernest as "the loneliest man in the building," forgotten by his former Labor associates. According to an office worker Booker interviewed, my grandfather simply sat at his desk and "shuffled papers" all day.[46]

Devastated by ill health and haunted by a sense of failure, J. Ernest finally drafted a letter resigning his position. On July 7, 1958, he sent a short memo to Mitchell: "Attached hereto is a copy of letter which I am sending to the President. I am sure you are aware of its subject matter." In his letter, J. Ernest gives "personal considerations" as the reason for his resignation. Secretary Mitchell immediately sent Eisenhower suggestions for a presidential letter accepting the resignation and began making plans for J. Ernest's replacement.[47]

Not long beforehand, Secretary Mitchell had had a run-in with NAACP representative Clarence Mitchell at a news conference. E. Frederick Morrow and other insiders speculated that the labor secretary's dismissal of J. Ernest was a way of indicating that he had "had enough" of the civil rights issue.[48] It is probably more accurate to say that tension between Secretary Mitchell and my grandfather had been building for some time. Perhaps Mitchell's run in with the NAACP was simply the straw that broke the proverbial camel's back.

What is clear, however, is that Mitchell had already decided, J. Ernest's replacement would be a white man. While my grandfather had been selected for his position after years of distinguished professional service, his successor was little more than half his age with an extremely short resume. Perhaps the man's most important qualification was that he was the son of Eisenhower's close friend Ambassador Henry Cabot Lodge. For the past few months, the young George Lodge had been working as my grandfather's assistant. Now, he would take over my grandfather's job. Rumors of J. Ernest's impending departure flew all over Washington. On July 17, Morrow wrote in his diary:

The real story behind this is not available, although I understand that there have been personal differences between him and Secretary of Labor James Mitchell. Because of my official position here, I have been aware of the impending resignation and have even seen the proposed letters to be exchanged between the White House and Mr. Wilkins. . . . Present plans call for a friendly exchange of letters between Mr. Wilkins and the President, and Mr. Wilkins will come to the White House for a farewell with him. Then the exchange of correspondence between them will be given to the press.[49]

It was a polite dance, where face would be saved and an outcry from the black press would be avoided. But although J. Ernest's departure from the Labor Department was by now a certainty, he refused to leave gracefully. When White House Chief of Staff Sherman Adams attempted to meet with J. Ernest to discuss the matter, my grandfather refused. When Vice President Nixon offered to intervene, J. Ernest again refused, saying that he wanted to take his case directly to the president.[50] Just as he had refused to take orders from Mitchell's assistant in 1955, he now refused to discuss his resignation with anyone except the man at the top. Booker in *Ebony* quotes J. Ernest as saying, "The President appointed me and I want him to hear my case."[51]

In preparation for the president's meeting with my grandfather, Mitchell prepared some notes to brief Eisenhower on the situation. After summarizing J. Ernest's professional history with his department and giving the president some information about J. Ernest's family, Mitchell wrote: "Mr. Wilkins has suffered several illnesses during the past year and is presently undergoing treatment at Walter Reed Hospital. You might want to suggest that he could continue to receive treatment there."[52] My guess is that Mitchell was hoping the president could persuade my grandfather to use his recent stint in the hospital as an excuse to make a graceful exit.

On August 5, 1958, J. Ernest met with Eisenhower. The president's calendar for that day shows that J. Ernest was given exactly thirteen minutes to make his case. Ann Whitman, the president's secretary, took notes:

Honorable J. Ernest Wilkins, who has been Asst. Sec. of Labor. Apparently he was very emotional (he has been ill) and had wanted to stay on for another six months which would enable him to get a pension. Also, apparently, he is being forced to resign. Governor Adams sat in on the appointment and promised President he would try to find a spot for Mr. Wilkins so he could serve out the six months necessary.[53]

Syndicated columnist and Washington insider Drew Pearson wrote up the meeting in his weekly column, saying that my grandfather "wept" as he put his case before the president. According to Pearson, Eisenhower remained adamant. Cabinet members had the right to choose their own staff, and Mitchell was determined that J. Ernest must leave the Labor Department. My grandfather was not going to back down for anyone, however, not even the president. According to Pearson, "Wilkins told the President that he would think about the request for his resignation. Wilkins has been considered a rather mild-mannered man, and nobody expected him to hesitate over acceding to the President's request."[54]

Thirteen minutes later, the meeting was over. Shattered, his last options exhausted, my grandfather returned to his office to deliberate. Always a reserved, self-contained, and "proper" man, he had broken down in tears before the president of the United States. After pleading to hold on to his job, he had been told that he would have to go.

J. Ernest, now nearly sixty-five years of age, must have worried about how he would provide for his family. His position on the Civil Rights Commission, although prestigious, was an unpaid one. In order to collect a retirement pension, my grandfather needed to work as a civil servant for another five months. Although Sherman Adams promised to arrange this, I could find no indication that J. Ernest was given another civil service job after he left the Labor Department.

Surely this period must have been the nadir of my grandfather's life. His financial future was threatened. His professional life was in ruins, and he continued to be dogged with ill health. Still, typically tight-lipped, J. Ernest did not share his problems with his children. His wife, Lucile, must have known about his failing health but continued to pursue her own busy career as an in-demand public speaker and member of the United Methodist Women's Board.

Habits formed early in life are difficult to shake later on. Stoicism had gotten him through the hard times of his youth. Stoicism was what he fell back on in this time of crisis.

On August 20, 1958, Alice Dunnigan, the lone black reporter in the White House press corps, confronted Eisenhower at his weekly news conference: "Mr. President, would you care to comment on newspaper stories that the White House has asked J. Ernest Wilkins to resign his post as Assistant Secretary of Labor to make his position available to Mr. Lodge?"[55] Eisenhower acted as if he had not heard about the Lodge appointment, although it seems he must have known. After all, Frederick Morrow had known of it a full month before. Instead, the president told Dunnigan: "I will say this: I have had some talks with Secretary Wilkins, who was talking about the possibility that he might resign from that particular position in the Labor Department. I have never urged him to nor asked him to, or anything else."[56]

Perhaps not an outright lie, this surely was not the whole truth either. In the weeks that followed, the black press covered the story extensively. The *Pittsburgh Courier*'s headline for August 25 read, "Wilkins Told: 'Quit Little Cabinet Post,'" and included quotes from Pearson's column.[57] On August 30, Dunnigan repeated Eisenhower's response to her at the press conference and quoted Lodge as saying that the whole thing was just an "unfortunate rumor."[58]

Through it all, my grandfather maintained his tight-lipped demeanor. He could have whipped up the black press by commenting on his predicament. It wouldn't have taken much of a statement to create an incident. Instead, he declined to talk to reporters both before and after his meeting with the president. The *Baltimore Afro-American* continued the story on October 4, 1958, stating that, whereas Mitchell had announced Wilkins would be resigning for reasons of ill health, "Wilkins crossed up this formality by publicly denying that there was anything wrong with his health." The article mentions that Mitchell and my grandfather had had "differences of opinion" and went on to refer pointedly to Mitchell's run-in with the NAACP's Clarence Mitchell.[59] Finally, on November 6, 1958, using the same letter he had written four months earlier, a defeated J. Ernest formally submitted his resignation to the president. In a reply that had also been drafted months earlier, Eisenhower accepted his resignation, thanking him for his work with the ILO and hoping that he would continue on with the Civil Rights Commission.[60]

My grandfather's long ordeal was over, but many questions remained. The *Chicago Sun-Times* reported that "no mention of another appointment for Wilkins" was made. J. Ernest declined to comment on his future prospects, saying simply that he planned on "resting," after four and a half "strenuous years." Although he had fought desperately to hold on to his position, in the end my grandfather opted to leave without making a fuss. When asked if he had been forced to resign, he told reporters from the *Sun-Times* that his resignation was "entirely voluntary."[61]

The *Pittsburgh Courier* was not so sure, however. What particularly rankled was that J. Ernest had been asked to step aside for an inexperienced white man half his age: "Considering Mr. Wilkins' training and experience, it is unlikely that his former assistant would have succeeded him had he not been the UN Ambassador's son; having no other evident claim to fame." The *Courier* also pointed out that J. Ernest's expulsion from the Little Cabinet did not bode well for the future of the Civil Rights Commission. "It is suggestive of the role the

President's Civil Rights Commission is expected to play when an able public servant dropped as Assistant Secretary of Labor is nevertheless retained as a member of this important commission." The paper's editor spoke for many African Americans when he wondered, "Are other top Negro appointees to be sacrificed on the altar of political expediency?"[62]

My eyes filled with tears as I read the story of J. Ernest's departure from the Labor Department. I had barely known my grandfather, but in the past three years I'd come to feel very close to him. For most of the afternoon I'd been sitting in front of a microfilm reader helplessly watching the inexorable destruction of his hopes and dreams. It felt as though someone had punched me in the stomach. Collecting the many photocopies I had made from *Ebony*, I carefully rewound the microfilm, turned off the machine, and left the air-conditioned comfort of Fitchburg State's library. As I inched through the late afternoon traffic back toward Boston, I mulled over what I had read.

Was race a factor in my grandfather's forced resignation? In August 1958 an irate black voter who had read Drew Pearson's column wrote Secretary Mitchell to suggest exactly that. Inching along past a truck rollover in the breakdown lane, I smiled to myself as I remembered the woman's letter. "Don't you know I could hardly believe this when I read it," she wrote, referring to the Pearson article. "Of all the dirty underhand deals that the present administration has pulled, this is the worst I ever heard of. . . . I will say one thing you never would have put a white man out to put in a Negro, and this man Lodge. What has he got besides wealth and a prominent father[?]" Booker wrote in *Ebony* that, while race may not have played an overt role in J. Ernest's resignation, it "lurked in the shadows." Later, Jessie Carney Smith wrote an article about my grandfather as a man who, like so many others, had become "another black man at risk."[63]

The kind of prejudice that lurks in the shadows, however, can be very hard to see, particularly by people who are not too interested in looking for it in the first place. Secretary Mitchell's reply to Mrs. Herndon's letter was indignant. After stressing that J. Ernest had resigned for "personal considerations," he wrote, "What I cannot quite comprehend is your reasoning in attaching racial considerations to this matter. This has no bearing on the question, whatsoever; just as it had no bearing when Mr. Wilkins was originally selected." Mitchell continued:

For my own part, I must add that some of your assertions are a bit disappointing to one who has put a great deal of effort into urging employers around the nation to abandon any and all discriminatory hiring practices, and who has consistently and openly spoken out in opposition to racial segregation in the South. I, for one, cannot believe that the intelligence of the American Negro voter would permit him to have his judgment influenced by a false set of facts.[64]

As I turned off the crowded highway and circled down the steep curve of the exit ramp, I kept turning over in my mind all the things I had read that day. Although Mitchell's letter to Herndon had been sent more than fifty years ago, the whole exchange felt eerily contemporary. My guess is that for Mitchell, a man who did indeed support black civil rights efforts, the fact that my grandfather was not openly called a "nigger" on the job meant that race had not been a factor in his resignation. But Mitchell did not realize that race had everything to do with the kind of man my grandfather was—his lack of experience with labor unions, his inability to negotiate government bureaucracies effectively, his unwillingness to ask for help from his white colleagues, and his inability to function well in the clubby all-white environment at the Labor Department.

A white man of J. Ernest's abilities would not have been starting his first government job at the age of sixty. Had he been white, my grandfather would have had the benefit of mentors to teach him the ropes before he ever got into serious trouble with his boss. Had he been white, my grandfather would have been put in a position tailored to his unique abilities as a lawyer. Instead, because J. Ernest was not white, he was placed in the job where his race could be used to the greatest public relations advantage.[65] Describing his own bitter experiences as the lone black man on Eisenhower's White House staff, E. Frederick Morrow wrote, "I do not believe it is possible for a black to ever be fully accepted, without any reservation, into the power structure of this country. A black man may penetrate and be within the structure, but not of it."[66]

As I turned off Massachusetts Avenue into the relative quiet of the street where I lived, I wondered what Mr. Morrow would have thought about Barack Obama's presidential campaign. I am sure a man of Morrow's political experience would have had a lot to say about the way the issue of race has been handled by both sides during the campaign. Still in a pensive mood, I pulled the car into my driveway, turned the motor off, leaned my head against the steering wheel, and sat. As the effects of my car's air conditioning wore off, the air became thick, heavy, and still. Yet I continued to sit quietly, with the windows closed, as little beads of sweat crept down my neck and into my shirt.

I had finally gotten an answer to the question that had been driving me for over three years. As much as I ever would, I now knew what had caused my grandfather's departure from the Labor Department. And as well as anyone now living could, I think I now understood why the whole event had been so traumatic for him. To be honest, discovering the truth about my grandfather's resignation had also been painful for me. As I sat in my car that hot July afternoon, tears mingled with the drops of sweat coursing down my cheek.

Unlike his fellow "black first" E. Frederick Morrow, J. Ernest Wilkins left no memoir about his tenure as a government official. A tight-lipped and reserved man, J. Ernest refused to discuss his resignation with the press. But in his quiet way, my grandfather had been a fighter. Although he was no longer part of the Labor Department, he continued his career in public service.

Rousing from my sweaty reverie, I unbuckled my seat belt, dug out a tissue from the glove compartment, wiped my eyes, and got out of the car. As I imagined what J. Ernest might have said about the tears I was now shedding, I had to smile. If I had in the last three years learned anything at all about my grandfather, it was that he did not indulge in self-pity. If J. Ernest had been sitting in the car with me at that moment, he would have reminded me that, although he had left the Labor Department, his most significant career accomplishment was still ahead.

Portrait of Assistant Secretary J. Ernest Wilkins, c. 1958

Chapter Fifteen

The Civil Rights Commission, 1957–1958

"So, Carolyn. What are you going to do with all this stuff?"

My sister-in-law Ann Marie poked a slender brown finger at the newspaper clippings I had laid out on the dining-room table and repeated her question.

"Really, Carolyn. This is great. You should think about writing this all down and publishing it."

I had been keeping track of my research adventures in a diary, and I'd roughed out some notes on J. Ernest's early life, but I hadn't given much thought at all to what would become of all the information I was compiling.

"I don't know, Annie," I said. "I'm a jazz musician. Writing a book seems like a pretty big project."

"It's not that hard, Carolyn." My sister-in-law is nothing if not persistent. "People do it all the time. Will you at least think about it?"

Well, she had me there. "OK, Annie. It's a great idea. I'll think it over."

I'd been having dinner at my brother David's house and listening to him and Ann Marie tell me about their adventures at the 2008 Democratic National Convention. The couple had actually gotten to say hello to Michelle Obama just minutes before her husband accepted the nomination.

"These are amazing times, Carolyn," David said, pouring us each another glass of wine. "A black man is running for president. Our grandfather would have been absolutely flabbergasted. When he was alive, there were still lots of places in this country where a black man couldn't even vote, let alone run for president."

Ann Marie and I nodded our heads in agreement as David swirled his wine pensively around in his glass.

"Carolyn, if you do write a book, be sure to write about J. Ernest's time on the Civil Rights Commission. He was the only black man on the very first commission in 1957. In a very real way it's fair to say the foundation for Obama's candidacy was laid by the work of that commission."

It's times like these when I remember that my brother is a professor at Harvard Law School. David continued, "That commission was created by the Civil Rights Act of 1957, which paved the way for the more comprehensive civil rights legislation passed by Congress in 1964. The 1957 Civil Rights Commission was America's first attempt to create a watchdog group to protect a lot of the freedoms we as black people enjoy today. And our grandfather was there, right at the center of it."

I had already done some reading about J. Ernest's work with the Civil Rights Commission. But until my brother brought it up, I hadn't really thought a lot about its larger historical context. Driving home, later that evening, I mulled over what Ann Marie had asked me. What was I going to do with all this stuff? I had tracked John Bird Wilkins across four states and documented his turbulent career as a Baptist preacher. I had followed his son J. Ernest's rise from a single-parent home in poverty to a position of power and influence in the upper echelons of American government. And most recently, I had uncovered the circumstances surrounding his abrupt departure from his precedent-setting position as Assistant Secretary of Labor. Perhaps it would be a good idea to document my research in a book, if only so that my great-grandchildren might have some idea who their people were.

But there was no point worrying too much about any future plans until I'd gathered all the necessary information. It was already the beginning of September. I had promised John I would wrap up my research before the end of the month. It was time to get busy. A week later, I made another trip to Widener Library in Harvard Yard.

A civil rights bill had been approved by Congress and signed into law on September 9, 1957, after months of arm-twisting by Senator Lyndon B. Johnson and a last-ditch filibuster by South Carolina's Strom Thurmond. An important provision of the bill required the president to create a bipartisan commission in order to investigate allegations of racial discrimination. To encompass what he called the "full spectrum" of points of view on the civil rights issue, President Eisenhower appointed an equal number of northern and southern representatives to the group.[1] No women were asked to join the commission. And, with the exception of my grandfather, all the commissioners were white.[2]

To represent the North, the president chose J. Ernest Wilkins, Michigan University president John Hannah, and the Reverend Theodore Hesburgh, a Jesuit priest, the president of Notre Dame University, and a strong civil rights advocate. Representing the southern point of view were Florida's former governor Doyle Carleton, Southern Methodist University Law School's dean Robert Storey, and Virginia governor John Battle. An avid segregationist, Battle believed that separation of the races was "the only answer to the Negro problem."[3]

The nation's press greeted the formation of the Civil Rights Commission with cautious optimism. *Time Magazine* called the new commissioners "earnest and judicially minded men" and predicted that they would have "considerable influence." The *Nation*, however, was not so sure. Since the six members were "deliberately chosen for their devotion to the cause of moderation, the Commission is not likely to break many lances crusading for civil rights," it speculated.[4] Writing in the *New Leader*, the black journalist Lewis Lomax was cautious. While J. Ernest was "no Uncle Tom," he was not known as a militant in the fight for civil rights. As for the commission, Lomax felt, it "may yet produce some good, not because of its intrinsic merit but because public opinion will not let it fail," a statement that fell somewhere between a ringing endorsement and a complete condemnation.[5]

Out of the vast sea of civil rights violations clamoring for immediate attention, the decision was made to focus the commission's initial hearings on instances where black citizens were being denied the right to vote. The idea that a person's right to vote should not be contingent on his race had broad support among white as well as black Americans. Nonetheless, the new commission encountered stiff resistance from southern congressmen, who delayed the group's funding and subjected its new staff director to a brutal and time-consuming confirmation process.[6]

It was late in the summer of 1958 before the commission began to meet regularly. The meetings were held behind closed doors, but rumors of contention within the group soon surfaced. John Hannah, often asked to play the peacemaker, told reporters that "at times it appeared it was going to be very difficult, indeed, to make real progress."[7]

The source of the disagreement involved the commission's choice of staff members. J. Ernest fought hard to ensure that African Americans were represented on the commission's staff. In *And Justice for All*, the historian and former commissioner Mary Frances Berry notes that my grandfather "had been particularly galled by the employment discrimination experiences of his son, Dr. J. Ernest Wilkins, Jr.," who, despite his PhD from the University of Chicago, had been "denied appointment at any research university because of his race."[8]

Today, it's hard to imagine why having black staff members on a commission dedicated to civil rights would be an issue. How could anyone investigate discrimination effectively using a group that excluded blacks from its staff? But, I had to keep reminding myself, this conflict was taking place in the 1950s. At the time there were probably twenty states in the Union where I could legally be denied the right to use a public toilet. My grandfather did not want to be the only black man involved in the commission's investigations, and he clashed repeatedly on this issue with segregationist governor John Battle. Despite his reputation as a "civil rights moderate," J. Ernest held his ground, and two African Americans were eventually added to the commission's investigating team.[9]

Over the next several weeks, commission staffers subpoenaed witnesses and heard the complaints of ninety-one African Americans who testified that they had been denied the right to vote because of their race. Just one month after his traumatic resignation from the Department of Labor, my grandfather and the rest of the commission members traveled to Montgomery, Alabama, to begin the first in a highly publicized series of hearings into allegations of voting rights violations in that state.

Before the group had even interviewed a single witness, the new commissioners got a chance to experience the "Southern way of life" firsthand. In a front-page story on December 4, 1958, the *New York Times* reported that, because my grandfather was with the group, Montgomery's segregated hotels refused to admit the commissioners. Commission member Reverend Theodore Hesburgh recalls that, on their first night in Montgomery, the group went to every hotel in town, knowing that they would be turned away. As a commission spokesman told reporters, "we wouldn't request rooms for some commissioners and not for all," and so the men were forced to stay at Maxwell Air Force Base, two miles from the city.[10]

When I interviewed him by phone, Reverend Hesburgh said that, when the exhausted and irritated commissioners arrived at Maxwell Air Force Base, the captain on night duty informed them that J. Ernest's quarters would not be in the same area as those of the white commission members. Commission member John Hannah was furious. "Give me the phone," he barked at the young officer. "Put me through to the president!"

Hannah told Eisenhower, "You gave us a tough job to do!" and explained that the air force was trying to put J. Ernest in segregated quarters. According to Father Hesburgh, the president then ordered that the base commander be brought to the phone immediately. By the time the general in charge had been located, Rev. Hesburgh told me, all the air force men were "quaking in their boots."[11]

When the base commander finally came to the phone, he got an earful from his commander in chief. Eisenhower told the general that if he didn't give the commissioners rooms and a desegregated place to eat, the man would be "in Timbuktu the next morning." Rev. Hesburgh recalls with grim satisfaction that Eisenhower "scared the wits out of that general." When it was all over, the weary commissioners were finally able to get a decent meal together and a place to sleep.[12]

The City of Montgomery's refusal to provide a hotel room for a black man, even a high-profile black man traveling on a mission from the president of the United States, was an ominous indication of southern attitudes. Judge George

Wallace had already defied a federal subpoena that ordered him to turn over the voting records for two Alabama counties. A virulent segregationist who would later run for president as a third-party candidate, Wallace refused to testify before the commission and threatened to jail any federal agent who attempted to retrieve the contested voting records. On December 9, 1958, spectators crowded into the small courtroom to watch the commission's first day of hearings. The tension in the room was palpable. In order to keep the proceedings from being interrupted by unruly spectators, Chairman Storey was forced to call for order repeatedly.[13]

One by one, twenty-seven African Americans took the witness box to describe the discriminatory methods used by Alabama officials. Amelia Adams, a soft-spoken graduate student at Tuskegee University, told the commissioners that when she went to the courthouse and announced her intention to register, she was told to copy Article Two of the U.S. Constitution in its entirety, without any mistakes and in clear penmanship. After she submitted the eight-and-a-half-page document as requested, Adams waited for months to hear whether she had been added to Alabama's voting rolls. She never received a reply from the state.

From his position among the commissioners on the speakers' platform, my grandfather questioned her.

"Do you have any opinion as to the reason why you haven't heard from it?"

"Well, I can read, I can write, and I think I possess all my mental facilities. So the only thing I can think of is the fact that I am a Negro," Adams replied.[14]

As the hearings progressed, a rogues' gallery of Alabama officials paraded before the commission claiming to be utterly in the dark as to why no blacks were registered to vote in their counties. When Probate Judge Varner from Macon County stood before the committee to testify, he played up his "cornpone homeboy" image to the hilt. When asked why no blacks appeared on his voting rolls, Varner replied that he "only kept the records" and otherwise had no idea of what was going on. My grandfather pressed Varner to explain the procedure used for filling out the registration forms. In his best "Bubba" manner, Varner replied, "I don't know how they fix the papers. I don't even remember what's on the paper. It's been so long since I looked at one."[15]

Commissioner Battle then asked Varner if there were different registration forms for black and white voters. "Not so far as I know," Varner replied. But my grandfather was not in the mood for Varner's evasive tactics. It was impossible for Varner to say that whites and blacks followed the same registration procedures, J. Ernest observed acidly. "He never saw the records, never saw the applications, and was never present in the registration room!"[16]

Booker writes in *Ebony* that my grandfather's handling of the witnesses impressed a black reporter who attended the hearing. "There is not an ounce of fear in Wilkins. He is sharp. Where has he been all this time?" Booker also quotes another eyewitness as saying that J. Ernest "plunged right in and hit the heart of the matter. Being a Negro, he upset the tradition in that area for years to come."[17]

Of the fourteen Alabama officials called before the Civil Rights Commission that day, six refused to testify at all. The rest steadfastly maintained their total ignorance of registration procedures. When my grandfather asked a Lownes County probate judge if he considered it odd that none of the fourteen thousand blacks in his county had registered to vote, the judge admitted that the situation might be considered "a little unusual, peculiar in some places, even."[18]

By the end of the second day of testimony, the Montgomery hearings had reached an impasse. The state of Alabama refused to acknowledge the commission's authority to subpoena documents. Even Governor John Battle, an avowed segregationist, was frustrated. As the second afternoon's session came to a close, Battle told the recalcitrant state officials that he believed segregation was "[t]he right and proper way of life in the South." But, he continued, their refusal to cooperate with the federal government was "an error."[19]

Although they did not have full access to Alabama's voting records, the commission's hearings had exposed numerous instances of racial discrimination by state election officials. In order to keep blacks off the voting rolls, Alabama registrars did not publish voter registration times or places. When registration sessions were scheduled, the sessions for black voters would be held in tiny rooms that could not contain all the applicants. Alabama officials often required black applicants to fill out overly complicated forms and to wait in lines for hours at a time. And as my grandfather discovered during his questioning of Amelia Adams, a popular tactic used by Alabama officials involved having black applicants copy an article of the constitution perfectly or be disqualified from voting.[20]

As 1958 drew to a close, my grandfather must have been exhausted. In the past year he had waged a bitter and humiliating battle to hold on to his job. He had suffered a major heart attack that nearly cost him his sight. Now he was trying to represent his race in a high-profile attempt to eliminate discrimination at the ballot box in the South. At Wilkins family gatherings, however, J. Ernest kept his troubles to himself. I find it hard to believe, but my mother assures me that neither the subject of J. Ernest's resignation nor that of his failing health was ever discussed. Perhaps my grandfather's stoic midwestern values would not allow him to complain while there was still so much work to be done. Or perhaps his pain was just too large for discussion.

In January 1959, the Civil Rights Commission returned to Montgomery, Alabama, for further hearings. Although less dramatic than the first session, these hearings continued to gather solid evidence of discriminatory tactics aimed at black voters. More important, the commission's hearings exposed Alabama's racist practices to nationwide scrutiny. The commission's findings shocked many whites, including the president, who called the behavior of the Alabama officials "reprehensible."[21]

Under the new civil rights legislation, Alabama's efforts to deny the vote to blacks were illegal. At the end of the second round of hearings, John Hannah, now the commission's chairman, announced that he would turn the commission's findings over to the Justice Department's new Civil Rights Division. My grandfather pushed the commission members to make an even stronger recommendation, but he was opposed by Governor Battle, who preferred that the commission take no further action. In the end a compromise measure was approved, and the case against the state of Alabama was referred to the Justice Department.[22]

In response to the commission's request, the Justice Department filed a suit in federal court requesting access to Alabama's voting records. The state of Alabama promptly responded by passing a law authorizing the immediate destruction of all rejected voter applications. The Civil Rights Commission then recommended that the federal government provide registrars for all elections to ensure equal access to the ballot box. But this proposal failed to attract the active support of Eisenhower officials. When Hannah tried to arrange a presentation by commission members to the Cabinet, Eisenhower's chief of staff, Wilton B. Persons (an Alabama native), somehow "forgot" to schedule a meeting, confirming the suspicions of some commissioners that the administration was not interested in a vigorous follow-up of the commission's recommendations.[23]

Years later, White House aide E. Frederick Morrow wrote in his memoirs that Eisenhower's "lukewarm" stand on civil rights had made him "heartsick." The attitude of administration officials was, he felt, "the greatest cross I had to bear during my eight years in Washington."[24] J. Ernest left us no record of his feelings on the subject. It is easy for me to suspect, however, that at some level my grandfather felt betrayed.

In his journal entry for October 20, 1957, Morrow wrote that he felt "ridiculous standing on platforms all over the country, trying to defend the Administration's record on Civil Rights." In spite of Eisenhower's decision to place blacks in high-profile positions, Morrow felt, there was no "strong, clarion and commanding voice from the White House" speaking out in support of civil rights issues. At the same time, Morrow often felt the black press viewed him as a "traitor" because of his involvement with an administration that had made "many blunders" in the area of race relations.[25]

My grandfather had also come under fire from the black press during the course of his work on the commission. On August 2, 1958, the *Amsterdam News* reported that Commissioner Robert Storey had given a five-hundred-dollar campaign contribution to a segregationist candidate in Texas. New York congressman Adam Clayton Powell, an outspoken civil rights advocate, demanded that Storey resign from the commission. In a fiery editorial, the *Amsterdam News* took the rhetoric a step further. If Storey would not step aside, the newspaper felt that J. Ernest Wilkins, as black America's only representative on the commission, should resign his position in protest.[26] The fact that this incident blew over without either my grandfather or Storey resigning speaks to the kind of iron self-restraint black "moderates" were expected to exercise during those times.

Although he probably felt discouraged and must have been bone-tired, J. Ernest kept up his daunting schedule. The Civil Rights Commission had begun to investigate voter discrimination in Shreveport, Louisiana, and a new round of hearings was scheduled to begin during the summer of 1959.[27] In addition to the Civil Rights Commission, my grandfather remained active in numerous organizations. He was on the board of Chicago's Provident Hospital and of the Hyde Park Kenwood Association, and he was the chairman of St. Mark's building fund. Heavily involved in the work of Kappa Alpha Psi fraternity, my grandfather also belonged to three other fraternal organizations, the Knights of Pythias, Sigma Pi Phi, and the Masons. In 1956 he made history as the first African American to be elected president of the Methodist Judicial Council.[28]

But J. Ernest was not well. Although he refused to complain, his constant traveling, heavy workload, and the traumatizing events of the past year had all taken a toll on his health. Sometime in the wee hours of Monday, January 19, 1959, after returning home from a weekend speaking engagement, J. Ernest Wilkins suffered a massive stroke and died instantly. Lucile was out of town that weekend and was not at home when my grandfather died. When the housekeeper arrived the next morning, she found my grandfather dead in a massive pool of blood, his suitcases from the night before still unpacked.[29]

The following day, President Eisenhower issued a statement to the press in which he called my grandfather "a gifted and dedicated public servant." Labor Secretary Mitchell told reporters that "Mr. Wilkins advanced the welfare not only of our country's minority citizens, but that of all our citizens."[30]

Even in death, my grandfather was a racial pioneer, for his body lay in state at Washington's Foundry Methodist Church on January 21, 1959. J. Ernest Wilkins was the first African American ever to be accorded that honor.[31] On January 22, my father arranged for J. Ernest's body to be brought to Chicago by train, and on January 23 a large funeral was held for him at St. Mark Methodist Church. After the funeral, J. Ernest Wilkins was laid to rest in the family plot at Lincoln Cemetery, alongside Lucile's mother and grandmother. Six years later, Lucile would be buried beside him, dead of a stroke at the age of sixty-four. In

1984 J. Ernest's youngest son, Julian, my father, would also be interred in the family plot.

Lincoln, a historic African American cemetery, is located in Chicago's southwestern suburbs. Keeping my family company in eternity are a lot of famous African Americans including Louis Armstrong's wife, Lil Hardin Armstrong; Rube Foster, the founder of Negro League Baseball; and the Pulitzer Prize-winning poet Gwendolyn Brooks.[32] On a recent visit to Chicago, I took a solitary stroll through the cemetery's well-maintained grounds. After having seen the collapsed tombstones and overgrown graves that now comprised much of St. Louis's Washington Park Cemetery, I was thrilled to see that my grandfather's final resting place remains as beautiful now as it was fifty years ago. The Wilkins family plot is situated near an old weeping willow whose branches hang just a few feet above the ground. The cemetery still accepts new residents, and I spotted a number of expensive floral arrangements dotting the graves. Steps from where my grandfather is buried lie the graves of several distinguished Methodist pastors. As I bent to brush a stray leaf from his grave, I prayed that somewhere in heaven, J. Ernest was pleased with the research I had done.

My grandfather had been a highly private man, with several secrets buttoned tightly under his vest. In the course of the last three years, I had peeled away the layers of his life like an overripe onion. I had probed his pain and explored his greatest career failure. I had exposed his illegitimate birth and his father's bigamy.

I had chronicled his successes and documented his uncompromising intelligence. But I had also made public the damage his extraordinary emotional repression caused to the family psyche. My mother tells me that none of J. Ernest's sons cried at his funeral. This is not because they didn't love him but because, in moments of great emotional stress, Wilkins men for generations have been trained to repress their feelings.

As I took a seat on the soft grass next to my grandfather's grave, it occurred to me that our family's extraordinary emotional disconnect had probably gone all the way back to the days of slavery. My great-grandfather John Bird Wilkins must have witnessed an unspeakable amount of chaos, destruction, and death as a child. Perhaps turning his emotions off was an essential method of survival.

My great-grandfather was a brilliant man who, because of the racial discrimination that characterized the times in which he lived, had never been able to receive his due. If John Bird were alive today, he might well actually have gone to Harvard instead of having to make up all those lies. With his obvious intelligence, good looks, charisma, and gift for self-promotion, my great-grandfather might even have become the president of his class.

I could not respect John Bird for deserting my great-grandmother and her five children, yet I was not blind to the fact that my great-grandfather Wilkins had left his mark on each of us. Not only do all the Wilkins family members share his light skin, wavy hair, and bulbous nose, but somehow, across 150 years and four generations, we also share John Bird's desire to do something significant with our lives. My great-grandfather's dream of a People's Temple where black Christians of all denominations could worship together failed. But his spirit of idealism lived on in J. Ernest's determination to serve his country on our nation's first Civil Rights Commission.

And although my grandfather suffered severe setbacks on his journey, each of his sons has also made his own contribution to history. My grandfather's eldest son, J. Ernest Jr., is an extraordinary physicist, becoming a "black first" in so many areas that everyone in the family has stopped counting. J. Ernest's middle son, John, became the first black man on the faculty of University of California at Berkeley's prestigious Boalt School of Law. J. Ernest's youngest son, my father, Julian Wilkins, was the first African American to integrate a major Chicago law firm.

The desire to make our lives count for something still burns bright among the Wilkins children today. My brother David could have simply sat on his laurels as a tenured Harvard law professor, but he didn't. He went out and started a center for the study of the legal profession so that scholars could examine the issues of globalization now facing so many law firms. In his job at the Chicago Public Schools, my middle brother, Stephen, works hard to bring sports education to inner-city children. Timothy, my baby brother, has created a black lawyers' group to mentor young associates of color at his high-powered New York law firm.

And what about me? I managed to make a successful career as a college professor, but I suffered for many years from a lack of clarity about who I really was. Growing up in the clannish environment of Chicago's light-skinned elite, I'd developed a limited idea of what it meant to be a black person. Then, away at college during the rebellious black power era, I was forced to reinvent my concept. But underneath all the labels, who was I really?

After three years of research, I felt a lot closer to being able to answer that question. Now I knew at least some of the story of my ancestors. If I studied their achievements and their failures closely, I could see pieces of myself, for better or worse. Just as my great-grandfather John Bird and my grandfather J. Ernest, I feel driven to excel at whatever task I undertake. If I am honest with myself, I have to admit that, just like J. Ernest and John Bird, I am sometimes more concerned with my public image than I ought to be. Like both men, I'd like to think I also possess a healthy intellectual curiosity. I didn't inherit their abilities in mathematics or science, but I'm not too bad with words. Many times in the telling of this story, I thought of my great-grandfather, the self-professed "newspaper man."

Yes. There was just no question about it. I was John Bird Wilkins's great-granddaughter. Light and bright perhaps, but definitely not white.

As I continued to sit by J. Ernest's grave, the strangest urge came over me. At first, I repressed it. After all, I was in a public graveyard. But a little voice inside kept saying: "Do it. Do it, please!"

I looked around furtively to see if anyone was standing nearby. But except for a man running a lawnmower several yards away, the coast was clear. I stood up and cleared my throat. Gesturing to my imaginary audience among the headstones, I began to speak in my best "nightclub performer" demeanor: "Good afternoon, ladies and gentlemen. I'd like to dedicate this next song to all you folks out there in Ancestor-land. It's an old African American spiritual. I am sure you all know it. But do me a favor please, ladies and gents. Don't scare me to death by singing along. I'm nowhere near ready to join you in the afterlife just yet."

I let out a nervous giggle, straightened my posture, and took a deep breath. And suddenly, just as she had many years ago, the Singer took me over. No longer concerned with anything but the music, I began to sing:

> There is a balm in Gilead
> That makes the wounded whole
> There is a balm in Gilead
> That heals the sin-sick soul
> Sometimes I feel discouraged
> And think my work's in vain
> But then the Holy Spirit
> Revives my soul again
> Revives my Soul again

As the last tones of the song died away, a deep and inexplicable feeling of connection enveloped me like the gentlest of mists. Whispering a last prayer of gratitude to God for the gift of life and for my amazing ancestors, I carefully placed a bouquet of roses beside my grandfather's grave and left the cemetery.

Clockwise from left: Stephen, Ann Marie, David, Timothy, Carolyn, and Aunt Marj, Easter Sunday, 1995

Epilogue

As I sit down to write these pages, I am reminded of a song by Bernard Ingner called "Everything Must Change". In the three years that have passed since I traveled to Missouri, circumstances have changed for some of the people and places I wrote about. After a lifetime of community activism, teaching, and nurturing her large extended family, Mrs. Ethel Porter passed away at age 101 last summer. Her grandson Chris, who generously shared his treasure trove of photos with me in the lobby of a motel near the St. Louis Airport, has left St. Louis to work at the U.S. Navy Hospital in Pensacola, Florida.

The Farmington Public Library has begun a major renovation of its Genealogy Room, and local interest in the town's African American history appears to be on the rise. Vonne Phillips Karraker, a black attorney and community activist, has started an organization dedicated to locating, identifying, and providing headstones for all the graves in the cemetery where my great-grandmother Susie Douthit is buried. I am especially pleased to learn that the Farmington Cemetery Preservation Association plans to install historic markers around the cemetery and at what Ms. Karraker calls "little known places of historical significance" around the area.

Fund-raising to pay for these projects has already begun. Ms. Karraker tells me that "The Mayor has been talking about the Cemetery in his monthly radio address, and two of our board members have shows on the local radio station, so we're getting good publicity, which should continue to generate interest well past February if we keep at it."[1] After reading Karraker's email I get the strong sense that Farmington's "can-do" spirit is as alive and well today as it was when my great-grandfather organized the Colored Working Men's Association back in 1885.

Mr. Bill Matthews, who served as the town's first black councilman in the 1980s, is also involved in the preservation effort. Mr. Matthews's family has lived in the area for generations and has maintained Colored Masonic Cemetery for more than thirty years. To honor the contributions of African Americans to Farmington's history, Mr. Matthews plans to build a memorial garden on the site where Farmington's last black church stood before it was demolished a few years ago.

Bill Matthews knew community stalwart Ethelean Cayce well, and, like my grandfather, grew up a few short blocks from both St. Paul's Church and Colored Hall. Mr. Matthews attended the one-room Douglas school on the outskirts of town where, like J. Ernest Wilkins and every other child of color in Farmington for two generations, he was taught by the legendary Miss Daisey Baker. And like my grandfather thirty-five years before, Mr. Matthews was legally barred from attending Farmington High School because of his race. Although he never met my grandfather, Mr. Matthews actually knew J. Ernest's older brother Byrd (John Bird's second son with Susie Douthit). As I listened to Mr. Matthews's leisurely Missouri twang over the phone, I could feel a tangible connection to the Farmington my grandfather would have known as a boy. When Mr. Matthews told me he used to earn his boyhood spending money by mowing my great-uncle Byrd's lawn with an old-fashioned push mower, I got goose bumps.

Doing the research for this book has put me in touch with a number of people who are working to uncover Farmington's African American history. LaDonna Garner, a local African American genealogist, has offered to help the association create a database to list all the people buried at Colored Masonic Cemetery. Jane Turner, another African American resident, has recently published a book about her family's experiences in nearby Bonne Terre at the turn of the last century.

In my own small way, I have also helped to awaken local interest in Farmington's African American past. When Vonne Phillips Karraker learned that the *Daily Journal Online* was planning to run a series of articles on the town's African American community, she put me in touch with Paula Barr, the *Journal*'s investigative reporter. As a result, I am pleased to report that in addition to the usual stories about Ethelean Cayce and Daisey Baker, those interested in Farmington's black history can read in their local paper about J. Ernest Wilkins and his journey from a one-room segregated schoolhouse to the highest government position then available to an African American.[2]

I have a pretty good idea what my Aunt Marjory would say about all these new developments. If I close my eyes and get quiet for a minute, I can picture her nodding her head in satisfaction, a mischievous grin lifting the corners of her mouth. She whispers: "Now you see why I used to talk so much about Jeremiah and the rest of the ancestors. I may have stretched the truth a bit here and there, but as you know, storytelling is an art, not a science. The important thing is that I sparked your imagination, got you interested, and kept our story alive!"

The arc of history is long, and some dramas take lifetimes to unfold. To paraphrase James Weldon Johnson's hymn *Lift Every Voice and Sing* (known to an older generation as the "Negro National Anthem"), black people in America have traveled a road bathed in blood and watered with tears. Those of us who survive must not forget the persevering spirit exemplified by our ancestors during their long march into the twenty-first century. If we fail to share our stories with the next generation, this spirit will be lost. Which is why I've begun teaching my daughter this spiritual I learned from my mother when I was a little girl:

> Ain't gonna let nobody turn me around
> Turn me around
> Turn me around
> Ain't gonna let nobody turn me around
> I'm gonna hold out—
> Until my change comes

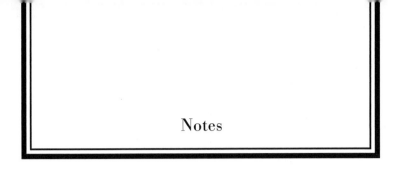

Notes

Chapter 1

1. E. Franklin Frazier, *Black Bourgeoisie*, 195.

Chapter 3

1. Jessie Carney Smith, "J. Ernest Wilkins," in *Notable Black American Men*.

2. W. Sherman Savage, *History of Lincoln University*, 134–35.

3. J. Ernest Wilkins, "Toastmaster's Address," presented during Lincoln University Founders' Day Celebration, Lincoln University, Jefferson City, 1941.

4. Ibid.

5. Arnold G. Parks, *Lincoln University, 1920–1970*, 89.

6. Wilkins, "Toastmaster's Address."

7. "Mann Loses Suit When Jury Verdict Favors Mrs. Spang," *University of Illinois Daily Illini (Urbana-Champaign)*, November 19, 1927.

8. Kappa Alpha Psi Fraternity, *A Short Chronicle of Kappa Alpha Psi Fraternity—A Brief History*, at http://www.kappaalphapsi1911.com/fraternity/history.asp, accessed February 21, 2009.

9. "J. Ernest Wilkins," *Who's Who in America, 1952–1953*.

10. Michael Washington and Cheryl Nunez, "Education, Racial Uplift and the Rise of the Greek-Letter Tradition," in *African American Fraternities and Sororities: The Legacy and Vision*, ed. Tamara L. Brown, Gregory S. Parks, and Clerenda M. Phillips, 139.

11. Kappa Alpha Psi Fraternity, *A Short Chronicle*.

12. Chad Williams, "Battle Scarred: World War I, African American Officers, and the Fight for Racial Equality," *Africana Heritage* 8 (2008): 8–9.

13. Molly Billings, "The Influenza Pandemic of 1918," *Human Virology at Stanford*, at http://virus.stanford.edu/uda/, accessed February 21, 2009.

14. "A Chronology of African American Military Service," at *http://www.AfricanAmericans.com/MilitaryChronology3.htm*, accessed February 21, 2009.

15. Ibid.

16. Eric Lawson and Jane Lawson, "Black Yankee: An Interview with Thomas Davis, First World War Veteran," at http://worldwarI.com/sfdavis, accessed February 21, 2009; Smith, "J. Ernest Wilkins."

17. Williams, "Battle Scarred," 8–9.

18. Roi Ottley, "See Wilkins' Post New Aid to Race," *Chicago Tribune*, May 2, 1954.

19. J. Hockley Smiley, "Mrs. Jack Johnson Laid to Rest Saturday, Thousands See Funeral," *Chicago Defender*, September 21, 1912.

Chapter 4

1. University of Chicago Registrar, "College Transcript for J. Ernest Wilkins Jr."
2. Laranita Dougas, telephone interview, December 18, 2008.
3. Constance Wilkins, telephone interview, June 15, 2008.
4. Ibid.
5. Dougas interview.

Chapter 5

1. http://www.HeritageQuest.com., accessed May 23, 2007
2. Evangeline Roberts, "Old Harvard Grad Speaks at Bethesda," *Chicago Defender,* October 29, 1927.
3. "The First Sermon of the Rev. Bird Wilkins," *Chicago Tribune,* April 18, 1887.
4. "A Dissenting Colored Baptist," *Chicago Tribune*, September 16, 1887.
5. Roberts, "Old Harvard Grad."
6. "Hold Funeral Services for Rev. J. D. Wilkins," *Chicago Defender,* August 20, 1938; "Rev. J. B. Wilkins of St. Louis, Yale Graduate, Buried," *St. Louis Argus,* August 12, 1938.
7. Roberts, "Old Harvard Grad."
8. "William Wilkins," *U.S. Census for Lafayette County, Mississippi,* 1870.
9. "John Wilkins," ibid.
10. Joel Williamson, *William Faulkner and Southern History*, 109.
11. "W. H. Wilkins," *U.S. Census for Lafayette County, Mississippi,* 1860.
12. Evelyn Crocker, "Slave Records of Lafayette County MS," MsGenWeb Project, at http://www.theusgenweb.org/ms/lafayette/slave_records.html, accessed February 21, 2009.
13. Don H. Doyle, *Faulkner's County: The Historical Roots of Yoknapatawpha*, 132–33.
14. Ibid, 132.
15. Ibid.
16. Ibid., 128–29.
17. Ibid., 134.
18. George P. Rawick, Jan Hillegas, and Ken Lawrence, *The American Slave: A Composite Autobiography*, 10:1925–31.
19. Doyle, *Faulkner's County*, 226.
20. Heather Williams, *Self-Taught: African-American Education in Slavery and Freedom,* 205, 18.
21. Roberts, "Old Harvard Grad."
22. Doyle, *Faulkner's County,* 269–70.
23. Edward Mayes, *History of Education in Mississippi*, U.S. Bureau of Education, 1899, at http://books.google.com/books?id=MRycAAAAMAAJ&printsec=frontcover&dq=edward +mayes&source=gbs_book.
24. Hollis Crowder, personal interview, January 8, 2009.
25. Anne Percy, *The Early History of Oxford, Mississippi*, 116–17.
26. Roberts, "Old Harvard Grad."
27. Doyle, *Faulkner's County,* 147.
28. Ibid., 284.
29. "Wilkins Is Persecuted: The Pastor of Liberty Church in Hard Lines," *Chicago Tribune*, January 6, 1888.
30. Doyle, *Faulkner's County,* 268.

Chapter 6

1. J. B. Wilkins deposit records, Memphis branch, Freedman's Bank Records, National Archives, Washington, D.C.

2. Joan Hassell, ed., *Memphis, 1800–1900,* 3:24, 22.

3. Ibid., 27, 24.

4. Bobby L. Lovett, "Beale Street," *Tennessee Encyclopedia of History and Culture.*

5. Williams, *Self-Taught,* 94.

6. Ibid., 36.

7. James W. Garner, *Reconstruction in Mississippi,* 359.

8. Williams, *Self-Taught,* 110–41.

9. Ibid., 161.

10. "J. B. Wilkins," *Memphis City Directory, 1874.*

11. J. B. Wilkins deposit records, Memphis branch, Freedman's Bank Records, National Archives, Washington, D.C.

12. Anne S. Butler, "Black Fraternal and Benevolent Societies in Nineteenth-Century America," 74–78.

13. Bobby L. Lovett, *The African-American History of Nashville, Tennessee, 1780–1930,* 112–13.

14. Reginald Washington, "The Freedman's Savings & Trust Company and African American Genealogical Research," *Federal Records and African American History* 29 (Summer 1997), at http://www.archives.gov/publications/prologue/1997/summer/freedmans-savings-and-trust.html, accessed February 21, 2009.

15. Hassell, *Memphis, 1800–1900,* 3:73, 79.

16. J. B. Wilkins and Susie Frierson, marriage certificate, Lafayette County, Mississippi.

17. The Web site was Ancestry.com.

18. Leroy Wilkins, death certificate, February 22, 1952, St. Louis County, Missouri.

19. "J. B. Wilkins," *U.S. Census for Lafayette County, Mississippi,* 1880.

20. Crowder interview.

Chapter 7

1. Roberts, "Old Harvard Grad."

2. Patrick Thompson, *History of the Negro Baptists in Mississippi;* J. A. Whitted, *History of the Negro Baptists of North Carolina;* William Hicks, *History of Louisiana Negro Baptists from 1804 to 1914.*

3. Ethelean Casey (Cayce), "History of the Black People in Farmington," *St. Francois Historical Society Newsletter,* June 27, 1984, in Fay Sitzes, ed., "African American History in Farmington."

4. Missouri Digital Heritage Timeline, at http://www.sos.mo.gov/archives/resources/africanamerican/timeline/, accessed January 20, 2009.

5. *St. Francois County Democrat,* July 21, 1887, quoted in St. Francois County Historical Society Newsletter, July 2008.

6. Ibid.

7. Ibid.

8. Karen K. Strait, "139-Year-Old Building Here Once Was Center of Activity for Black Community," *Farmington Forum,* February 14, 1996, in Sitzes, "African American History in Farmington."

9. Cayce, "Black People in Farmington."

10. "Hilliard Douthit," *U.S. Census for St. Francois County, Missouri*, 1880; "Colored Churches," *Farmington News*, October 14, 1927, in Sitzes, "African American History in Farmington."

11. "Interview with Ethelean Cayce," June 27, 1984, St. Francois Historical Society, in Sitzes, *African American History in Farmington.*

12. "First Sermon of the Rev. Bird Wilkins."

13. Photo of "Rev. Bird Wilkins," *Cleveland Gazette*, November 19, 1887.

14. Doyle, *Faulkner's County*, 154–56.

15. Thompson, *Negro Baptists in Mississippi*, 112.

16. Yusef Mgeni cited in Kathleen Cavett and Jill Hope, *Voices of Rondo: Oral Histories of Saint Paul's Historic Black Community*, 309.

17. Pilgrim Baptist Church, "History," at http://www.pilgrimbaptistchurch.org/history. htm, accessed January 30, 2008.

18. "Attention," *St Paul Western Appeal*, June 27, 1885.

19. "A Defense of Riel," *Christian Recorder*, December 10, 1885.

20. Paul Vibert, *La nouvelle France catholique.*

21. Pilgrim Baptist Church, "History."

22. "A New Pastor," *Chicago Daily Inter Ocean*, April 17, 1887.

Chapter 8

1. "A New Pastor."

2. "First Sermon of the Rev. Bird Wilkins."

3. Christopher Robert Reed, *Black Chicago's First Century*, 1:332.

4. "A Preacher on Sunday Legislation," City Page, *Chicago Tribune*, June 14, 1887.

5. Reed, *Black Chicago's First Century*, 1:241, 243.

6. "A Remarkable Sermon," *Chicago Tribune*, August 22, 1887.

7. Reed, *Black Chicago's First Century*, 1:318–20.

8. "Voice of the People," *Chicago Tribune*, August 26, 1887.

9. "Lagniappe," *New Orleans Daily Picayune*, September 4, 1887.

10. Reed, *Black Chicago's First Century*, 1:320.

11. Ibid.

12. "Wilkins Is Persecuted," *Chicago Tribune*, January 6, 1888.

13. "Pastor Resigns," *Chicago Daily Inter Ocean*, September 16, 1887.

14. "A Dissenting Colored Baptist," *Chicago Tribune*, September 17, 1887.

15. Ibid.

16. "Personal," *Philadelphia Christian Recorder*, October 13, 1887; "The First African Unitarian Church," *Milwaukee Sentinel*, October 10, 1887; "Other Christian Work," *Boston Congregationalist*, September 27, 1887.

17. "Rev. Bird Wilkins," *Cleveland Gazette*, November 19, 1887.

18. "Wilkins Is Persecuted," *Chicago Tribune*, January 6, 1888.

Chapter 9

1. Cayce, "Black People in Farmington."

2. John B. Wilkins, "Agricultural Machine," October 18, 1892, Washington, D.C.: U.S. Patent Office, at http://books.google.com/patents?id=2R52AAAAEBAJ&ie=ISO-8859-1, accessed February 21, 2009.

3. "Colored Churches."

4. "Rev. Bird Wilkins," in R. L. Polk and Company, *Little Rock, Arkansas City Directories, 1893–1898.*

5. "Everett Wilkins Draft Registration Card" in Missouri Soldiers' Database: War of 1812–World War I; "Howard Wilkins," U.S. Social Security Administration Death Index; "Howard R. Wilkins," *U.S. Census for Drew County, Arkansas,* 1900 (Bird is now calling himself Howard R. Wilkins, and his children are cited in this census record).

6. "Howard R. Wilkins," *U.S. Census for Drew County, Arkansas,* 1900.

7. "Susie Wilkins," *U.S. Census for St. Francois County, Missouri,* 1900.

8. David M. Katzman, *Seven Days a Week: Women and Domestic Service in Industrializing America,* 122.

9. "Hayward R. Wilkins," *U.S. Census for Ashley County, Arkansas,* 1910.

10. "Susie Wilkins," *U.S. Census for St. Francois County, Missouri,* 1910.

11. Tera Hunter, *To 'Joy My Freedom: Southern Black Women's Lives and Labors after the Civil War,* 57.

12. Cayce, "Black People in Farmington."

13. Hunter, *To 'Joy My Freedom,* 57.

14. Ibid.

15. Ibid.

16. "Susie Wilkins," *U.S. Census for St. Francois County, Missouri,* 1910.

17. "H. B. Wilkins Appointed by St. Louis Mayor," *Chicago Defender,* November 27, 1915.

18. J. C. Wright, letter to Carolyn Wilkins, May 8, 2008.

19. J. C. Wright, "Porter Family History, Jeffersonville, In." (unpublished manuscript). All further quotes in this chapter are from this manuscript.

Chapter 10

1. John A. Wright, Sr., *The Ville*: St. Louis, 7.

2. Ibid., 7–8.

3. Debra Foster Green, "Just Enough of Everything: The *St. Louis Argus,* an African American Newspaper and Publishing Company in Its First Decade," at http://www.hnet. org/~business/bhcweb/publications/BEHonline/2006/greene.pdf 3, accessed February 21, 2009.

4. Ibid.

5. Green, "Just enough of Everything," 5.

6. Dayse Baker, "Farmington Notes," *St. Louis Argus,* November 27, December 17, 1915, and January 7, 1916.

7. Green, "Just Enough of Everything," 5–6.

8. "The Clarion's Force Royally Entertained," *St. Louis Argus,* January 7, 1916.

9. "Rev. J. B. Wilkins of St. Louis."

10. "Howard B. Wilkins," *Gould's Directory for St. Louis,* 1919, 1920.

11. Wright, *The Ville,* 117–18, 17.

12. Benjamin Israel, "Oldest Black Newspaper in St. Louis on Last Legs," *St. Louis Journalism Review* (September 2003), at http://goliath.ecnext.com/coms2/summary_0199-3114442_ITM, accessed February 21, 2009.

13. "Howard B. Wilkins," *U.S. Census for St. Louis County,* 1920.

14. "Sixteen-Year-Old Linotypist Sets 40,000 Ems in Day," *St. Louis Argus,* March 30, 1923.

15. "Our Weekly Sermon," *Chicago Defender,* July 2, 1921.

16. Wright, *The Ville*, 7.

17. "Byrd J. Wilkins," *U.S. Census for St. Louis County*, 1920; "Everett H. Wilkins," Missouri Secretary of State, "Soldiers Database: War of 1812–World War I," at http://www.sos.mo.gov.archives/soldiers/ accessed October 15, 2007.

18. Constance Wilkins, telephone interview, June 15, 2008.

19. Wright, *The Ville*, 46.

20. "Took Bonus Checks Out U.S. Mails," *Chicago Defender*, October 14, 1922.

21. "Sixteen-Year-Old Linotypist."

22. Kappa Alpha Psi Fraternity, Inc., "Laurel Wreath Commission," at http://www.kappaalphapsi1911.com/committees/laurel_wreath.asp, accessed February 21, 2009.

23. U.S. Department of the Interior National Parks Service, "National Register of Historic Places Registration Form for Antioch Baptist Church," at www.dnr.mo.gov/shpo/nps-nr/99001166.pdf, accessed February 21, 2009.

24. "Antioch Baptist Church Notes," *St. Louis Argus*, March 10, 1916.

25. Roberts, "Old Harvard Grad."

26. Ibid.

27. "Rev. J. D. Wilkins, Minister and Teacher," *Chicago Defender*, August 20, 1938.

28. Robert Chadwell Williams, *Horace Greeley: Champion of American Freedom*.

29. "Rev. J. B. Wilkins of St. Louis."

Chapter 11

1. Marcus Kirkland, "The Early History of Farmington" (Farmington News Printing Company, 1965), at www.rootsweb.ancestry.com, accessed April 30, 2008.

2. Ibid.

3. Farmington Public Library, ed., *Farmington, Missouri: The First 200 Years, 1798–1998*, 119.

4. Kirkland, "Early History," 1.

5. Bob Schmidt, "1850 St. Francois Co. Mo. Census (Slave Schedules)," in Sitzes, "African American History in Farmington."

6. Dayse Baker, "Famous Sons and Daughters," ibid.

7. Wayne Leeman, "Farmington Teacher's 51-Year Career," *St. Louis Post-Dispatch*, May 13, 1954, ibid.

8. "Colored Churches."

9. "Ethelean Casey [Cayce]," *Evening Press*, August 1998, in Sitzes, "African American History in Farmington."

10. Cayce, "Black People in Farmington."

11. "Susie Wilkins," *U.S. Census for St. Francois County Missouri*, 1910, 1920, 1930.

12. Cayce, "Black People in Farmington."

13. Strait, "139–Year-Old Building."

Chapter 12

1. Fox News Report, WFNX TV, March 21, 2007.

2. "CNN News Report," September 19, 2007, at http://www.cnn.com/2007/POLITICS/09/19/jackson.jena6/index.html, accessed February 21, 2009.

3. Elizabeth Wilkins, personal interview, August 22, 2008.

4. James Montgomery, telephone interview, August 5, 2008.

5. Ibid.

6. J. Ernest Wilkins Jr., telephone interview, December 1995.

7. Elizabeth Wilkins, personal interview, August 22, 2008.

8. Public Broadcasting Service, "The Rise and Fall of Jim Crow," at http://www.pbs.org/wnet/jimcrow/stories_events_birth.html, accessed November 20, 2009.

Chapter 13

1. George N. Leighton, telephone interview, September 20, 2008.

2. "J. Ernest Wilkins," *Encyclopedia of World Methodism*, 1960. (Lincoln became a university in 1921.)

3. "J. Ernest Wilkins Dead in Capital," *Chicago Daily News*, January 20, 1958.

4. David A. Nichols, *A Matter of Justice: Eisenhower and the Beginning of the Civil Rights Revolution*, 25.

5. Damon Stetson, "Eisenhower Bids Board Fight Bias," *New York Times*, August 20, 1953.

6. Nichols, *A Matter of Justice*, 35.

7. Ibid., 36.

8. "Atty Wilkins Urges Churches to Insist on Morality in Government," *Chicago Defender*, October 31, 1953.

9. Nichols, *A Matter of Justice*, 38.

10. Robert Frederick Burk, *The Eisenhower Administration and Black Civil Rights*, 64.

11. "An Excellent Appointment," *New York Times*, March 5, 1954.

12. "Three Defense Aides Get Higher Posts," *New York Times*, May 4, 1954.

13. Richard Lewis, "Ike's Selection of Wilkins a Heavy Blow at Bias," *Chicago Sun-Times*, March 8, 1954.

14. Lewis Lautier, "Cite GOP Error on Wilkins," *Chicago Defender*, March 20, 1954.

15. "Abbot Would Be Proud," *Chicago Defender*, March 20, 1954; "An Excellent Appointment," *New York Times*, March 5, 1954; Leeman, "Teacher's 51-Year Career."

16. "Labor Post Goes to Negro, First of Race in Sub Cabinet," *New York Times*, March 5, 1954.

17. Ulysses Boykin, "The Motor City," *Chicago Defender*, April 24, 1954.

18. Burk, *Black Civil Rights*, 69.

19. Judge Anna Diggs Taylor, letter to author, July 24, 2008.

20. *Chicago Defender*, June 5, 1954, 10.

21. "Wilkins Stymies Reds at Geneva," *Chicago Defender*, June 19, 1954.

22. Michael Krenn, *Black Diplomacy: African Americans and the State Department, 1945–1969*, 5.

23. "Wilkins Stymies Reds at Geneva."

24. Harold Keith, "How About Negro Labor Attys.?" *Pittsburgh Courier*, June 26, 1954.

25. "'U.S. Can Serve World'—Wilkins," *Pittsburgh Courier*, July 10, 1954.

26. "The Sum of the Whole," *Chicago Defender*, July 24, 1954.

27. J. Ernest Wilkins, letter to Lucile Wilkins, November 12, 1954.

28. Burk, *Black Civil Rights*, 85.

29. E. Frederick Morrow, *Black Man in the White House*, 258.

30. Burk, *Black Civil Rights*, 80.

31. Morrow, *Black Man in the White House*, 201.

32. Burk, *Black Civil Rights*, 70.

33. "J. Ernest Wilkins in Historic First," *Pittsburgh Courier*, August 21, 1954.

34. J. Ernest Wilkins, "New Horizons," *Boule Journal* 18, no. 1 (October 1954).

35. A. H. Raskin, "Two Hungarians Ousted by ILO," *New York Times*, June 27, 1956.

36. Burk, *Black Civil Rights*, 73–74.

37. Simeon Booker, "The Last Days of J. Ernest Wilkins," *Ebony Magazine* (March 1960): 141.

38. *Chicago Defender*, March 13, 1954.

39. Alan Paton, "The Negro in America Today: South African Novelist Alan Paton Dissects the Racial Situation in the South in the Year of *Brown v Board of Education*," at http://www.historymatters.gmu.edu/6337, accessed August 3, 2008.

Chapter 14

1. "The Murder of Emmett Till," *American Experience*, at http://www.pbs.org/wgbh/amex/till/index.html, accessed February 26, 2008.

2. Ibid.

3. Morrow, *Black Man in the White House*, 29, 30.

4. Burk, *Black Civil Rights*, 20.

5. Ibid., 31.

6. Levi Jolley, "Washington News Beat," *Pittsburgh Courier*, December 2, 1955.

7. Burk, *Black Civil Rights*, 153, 154.

8. Ibid., 158.

9. Ibid., 159.

10. Ibid., 160.

11. Morrow, *Black Man in the White House*, 219 (also 48).

12. Burk, *Black Civil Rights*, 160–61.

13. Constance Wilkins, telephone interview, June 15, 2008.

14. Harold Keith, "Who's Who in Labor," *Pittsburgh Courier*, March 3, 1956.

15. "Jobs for Negro Pushed," *New York Times*, April 8, 1956.

16. Henry P. Gudza, "James P. Mitchell: Social Conscience of the Cabinet," *Monthly Labor Review* (August 1991), at http://www.dol.gov/search/AdvSearch.aspx?agcoll=&taxonomy=&search_term=James+P.+Mitchell&Image1.x=0&Image1.y=0&Image1=Go&offset=0 24–25, accessed February 26, 2009.

17. Rocco Siciliano, *Walking on Sand*, 122.

18. Rocco Siciliano, telephone interview, September 11, 2008.

19. Siciliano, *Walking on Sand*, 122.

20. John Gilhooley, memo to Millard Cass, typed at the bottom of a copy of a memo from Gilhooley to J. Ernest Wilkins (hereafter Wilkins), April 6, 1955, James P. Mitchell Papers (hereafter Mitchell Papers).

21. Millard Cass, handwritten notation at bottom of undated memo from Gilhooley to Wilkins; Gilhooley memo to Wilkins, April 13, 1955; James Mitchell, handwritten note on memo to Gilhooley, April 12, 1955, all in Mitchell Papers.

22. Wilkins, "Statement on the Evaluation of the International Labor Programs," April 20, 1956, ibid.

23. Mitchell, memo to Wilkins, July 7, 1956, ibid.

24. Booker, "Last Days," 142.

25. Ibid.

26. Ibid., 143.

27. Burk, *Black Civil Rights*, 168.

28. Ibid., 171.

29. Morrow, *Black Man in the White House*, 159.

30. "Wilkins Assails Bigots as against 'Law, Order,'" *Pittsburgh Courier*, October 15, 1954.

31. Morrow, *Black Man in the White House*, 170.

32. Nichols, *A Matter of Justice*, 206, 205.

33. Burk, *Black Civil Rights*, 229.

34. Foster Rhea Dulles, *The Civil Rights Commission, 1957–1965*, 18.

35. Burk, *Black Civil Rights*, 230.

36. Morrow, *Black Man in the White House*, 174.

37. Mitchell, letter to Wilkins, March 12, 1958, Mitchell Papers.

38. *Notre Dame Alumnus* (March 1958): 18.

39. Wilkins memos, 1957, administrative file, Mitchell Papers.

40. Wilkins, "Discrimination in the Field of Employment and Occupation," April 25, 1958, administrative file, Mitchell Papers.

41. Wilkins, letter to Mitchell, May 9, 1958, ibid.

42. Wilkins, letter to Under Secretary, April 29, 1958, administrative file, ibid.

43. Booker, "Last Days," 143.

44. Ibid., 142.

45. Ibid., 143.

46. Ibid.

47. Mitchell, draft memo to Dwight D. Eisenhower, July 15, 1958, Mitchell Papers; Morrow, *Black Man in the White House*, 238.

48. Morrow, *Black Man in the White House*, 238.

49. Ibid.

50. Booker, "Last Days," 143.

51. Ibid.

52. Mitchell, draft letter to Eisenhower (undated), Mitchell Papers.

53. Ann Whitman, diary entry for August 5, 1958, Ann Whitman Papers, Dwight D. Eisenhower Library.

54. Drew Pearson, "Wilkins Ouster a Racial Setback," *Baltimore Sun*, August 18, 1958.

55. Eisenhower, news conference no. 213, August 20, 1958, at http://www.presidency.ucsb.edu/ws/index.php?pid=11178&st=&st1=, accessed February 21, 2009.

56. Morrow, *Black Man in the White House*, 238; Eisenhower, news conference no. 213.

57. "Wilkins Told: 'Quit Little Cabinet Post,'" *Pittsburgh Courier*, August 25, 1958.

58. "Deny Wilkins 'Out,'" *Pittsburgh Courier*, August 30, 1958.

59. "Not for Ill Health," *Baltimore Afro-American*, October 4, 1958.

60. Wilkins, letter to Eisenhower, November 6, 1958, and Eisenhower, letter to Wilkins, November 7, 1958, Wilkins administrative file, Eisenhower Papers.

61. "Wilkins Quits; Negro Cabinet Aid," *Chicago Sun-Times*, November 9, 1958.

62. "The Dropping of J. Ernest Wilkins," *Pittsburgh Courier*, November 22, 1958.

63. G. Herndon, letter to Mitchell, August 22, 1958, Mitchell Papers; Booker, "Last Days," 141; Smith, "J. Ernest Wilkins."

64. Mitchell, letter to Herndon, November 29, 1958, Mitchell Papers.

65. Burk, *Black Civil Rights*, 69.

66. Morrow quoted in ibid., 87.

Chapter 15

1. Burk, *Black Civil Rights*, 229.

2. "Senate Unit Backs Six for Rights Group," *New York Times*, March 4, 1958.

3. Foster Rhea Dulles, *The Civil Rights Commission, 1957–1965*, 20.

4. Ibid., 19.

5. Ibid., 21.

6. Burk, *Black Civil Rights*, 232, 204, 231.

7. Dulles, *Civil Rights Commission*, 28.

8. Mary Frances Berry, *And Justice for All: The United States Commission on Civil rights and the Continuing Struggle for Freedom in America* (New York: Knopf, 2009), 14.

9. Dulles, *Civil Rights Commission*, 28, 21; Booker, "Last Days," 144.

10. Theodore Hesburgh, telephone interview, September 11, 2008; "Civil Rights Commission to Shun Segregated Montgomery Hotels," *New York Times*, December 4, 1958.

11. Hesburgh interview.

12. Ibid.

13. Dulles, *Civil Rights Commission*, 33, 37.

14. Ibid., 35.

15. Ibid., 36.

16. Ibid.

17. Booker, "Last Days," 144.

18. Dulles, *Civil Rights Commission*, 37.

19. Ibid.

20. Burk, *Black Civil Rights*, 234.

21. Dulles, *Civil Rights Commission*, 39.

22. Burk, *Black Civil Rights*, 235; Dulles, *Civil Rights Commission*, 39–40.

23. Burk, *Black Civil Rights*, 235, 236, 239.

24. Morrow, *Black Man in the White House*, 299.

25. Ibid., 179, 198.

26. "Downright Deceit," *Amsterdam News*, August 2, 1958.

27. Burk, *Black Civil Rights*, 236.

28. Smith, "J. Ernest Wilkins"; "Wilkins, J. Ernest," *Encyclopedia of World Methodism*, 1960.

29. Constance Wilkins interview, June 15, 2008.

30. "J. Ernest Wilkins, Top Mitchell Aide," *Washington Post and Times Herald*, January 20, 1959.

31. Booker, "Last Days," 144.

32. Jim Tipton, "Lincoln Cemetery," at http://www.findagrave.com/php/famous.php?FScemeteryid=106612&page=cem, accessed February 21, 2009.

Epilogue

1. Vonne Phillips Karraker, email to Carolyn Wilkins, March 5, 2010.

2. Paula Barr, "They Made A Difference: Overcoming Obstacles, Leaving a Mark on County History." *Daily Journal Online*, February 26, 2010, at http://www.dailyjournalonline.com/news/local/article_e0cb88fc-ad62-56bd-82ab-443322ffffc9.html Accessed on April 27, 2010.

Bibliography

Archives

Boston Public Library, Boston, Massachusetts
Cook County Clerk's Office, Chicago, Illinois
   Birth Records
   Marriage Records
Drew County Clerk's Office, Monticello, Arkansas
Marriage Records
Dwight D. Eisenhower Library
   James P. Mitchell Papers
   Anne Whitman Papers
Farmington Public Library Genealogy Archive, Farmington, Missouri
   Colored Masonic Cemetery Burial Records
   St. Francois County Marriage Records
Fitchburg State University Library, Fitchburg, Massachusetts
Hennepin County Clerk's Office, Minneapolis, Minnesota
   Marriage Records
Itawamba County Clerk's Office, Fulton, Mississippi
   Marriage Records
Lincoln University Library, Jefferson City, Missouri
National Archives, Washington, D.C.
   Freedman's Bank Records
   U.S. Patent Office
Newberry Library, Chicago, Illinois
Pulaski County Clerk's Office, Little Rock, Arkansas
   Marriage Records
Schomburg Center for Research in Black Culture, New York, New York
Sigma Pi Phi Archives, New York, New York
Skipwith Historical Society, Oxford, Mississippi
   St. Peter's Cemetery Burial Records
   Lafayette County Record of Colored Marriages
   Educable Children Records for Lafayette County

St. Louis County Clerk's Office, St. Louis, Missouri
Marriage Records
    Death Records
St. Louis County Library, St. Louis, Missouri
Genealogy Archives
    Washington Park Cemetery Burial Records
St. Louis Public Library, St. Louis, Missouri
U.S. Department of Labor Archives, Wirtz Labor Library, Washington, DC
United Methodist Church Archives and History Center, Madison, New Jersey
University of Chicago Library, Chicago, Illinois
University of Illinois at Urbana Library, Urbana, Illinois
University of Illinois Circle Campus Library, Chicago, Illinois
University of Mississippi Library, Oxford, Mississippi
J. Ernest Wilkins Papers, Private Collection, Boston, MA

U.S. Federal Censuses

Drew County, Arkansas. Census, 1910
Lafayette County, Mississippi. Census, 1860, 1870, 1880.
————. Slave schedule, 1850, 1860.
Pulaski County, Arkansas. Census, 1900
St. Francois County, Missouri. Census, 1880, 1900, 1910, 1920
St. Louis County, Missouri. Census, 1920, 1930

Newspapers

Baltimore Afro-American
Chicago Daily Inter Ocean
Chicago Defender
Chicago Sun-Times
Chicago Tribune
Cleveland Gazette
Farmington Times
Los Angeles Times
New York Amsterdam News
New York Times
Pittsburgh Courier
St. Louis Argus
St. Louis Post-Dispatch
St. Paul Western Appeal
University of Illinois Daily Illini

City Directories

Chicago, Illinois, 1888-1889
Little Rock, Arkansas, 1893-1894
Memphis, Tennessee, 1874-1878
St. Louis, Missouri, 1915-1938

Personal Interviews

Crowder, Hollis. Personal interview. Skipwith Historical Society, January 8, 2009.
Dougas, Laranita. Telephone interview, December 18, 2008.
Hesburgh, Theodore. Telephone interview, September 11, 2008.
Leighton, George N. Telephone interview, September 20, 2008.
Montgomery, James. Telephone interview, August 5, 2008.
Siciliano, Rocco. Telephone interview, September 11, 2008.
Wilkins, Constance. Telephone interview, June 8, 15, 2008.
Wilkins, Elizabeth. Personal interview, Chicago, IL., August 21 and 22, 2008.
Wilkins, J. Ernest Jr. Telephone interview, December 15, 1995.

Print Sources

Berry, Mary Frances. *And Justice for All: The United States Commission on Civil Rights and the Continuing Struggle for Freedom in America*. New York: Alfred A. Knopf, 2009.
Booker, Simeon. "The Last Days of J. Ernest Wilkins." *Ebony Magazine* (March 1960).
Burk, Robert Frederick. *The Eisenhower Administration and Black Civil Rights*. Knoxville: University of Tennessee Press, 1984
Butler, Anne S. "Black Fraternal and Benevolent Societies in Nineteenth-Century America." In Tamara L. Brown, Gregory S. Parks, and Clerenda M. Phillips, eds., *African American Fraternities and Sororities: The Legacy and the Vision*. Lexington: University Press of Kentucky, 2005.
Carroll, Rebecca. *Saving the Race: Conversations on DuBois from a Collective Memoir of Souls*. New York: Random House, 2004.
Cavett, Kathleen, and Jill Hope. *Voices of Rondo: Oral Histories of Saint Paul's Historic Black Community*. Minneapolis: Syren Book Company, 2005.
Cayce [Casey], Ethelean. "History of the Black People in Farmington," *St. Francois Historical Society Newsletter*, June 27, 1984. In Faye Sitzes, ed., "African American History in Farmington."
"Civil Rights Commission to Shun Segregated Montgomery Hotels." *New York Times*, December 4, 1958.

"Colored Churches," *Farmington News,* October 14, 1927. In Sitzes, "African American History in Farmington."

Doyle, Don H. *Faulkner's County: The Historical Roots of Yoknapatawpha.* Chapel Hill: University of North Carolina Press, 2001.

Dulles, Foster Rhea. *The Civil Rights Commission, 1957-1965.* Ann Arbor: Michigan State University Press, 1968.

Eisenhower, Dwight D. *Mandate for Change.* Garden City: Doubleday, 1963.

———. *Waging Peace.* Garden City: Doubleday, 1965.

Farmington Public Library, ed. *Farmington, Missouri: The First 200 Years, 1798-1998.* Paducah: Turner Publishing, 2000. "The First Sermon of the Rev. Bird Wilkins." *Chicago Tribune,* April 18, 1887.

Frazier, E. Franklin. *Black Bourgeoisie.* New York: Macmillan, 1957.

Garner, James W. *Reconstruction in Mississippi.* Baton Rouge: Louisiana State University Press, 1968.

Graham, Lawrence Otis. *Our Kind of People: Inside America's Black Upper Class.* New York: HarperCollins, 1999.

Graves, John William. *Town and Country: Race Relations in an Urban-Rural Context, Arkansas, 1865-1905.* Fayetteville: University of Arkansas Press, 1990.

Hassell, Joan, ed. *Memphis, 1800-1900.* Vol. 1, *Years of Challenge, 1800-1860*; vol. 2, *Years of Crisis, 1860-1870*; vol. 3, *Years of Courage, 1870-1900.* New York: Nancy Powers, 1982.

Herring, Cedric, Verna Keith and Hayward Horton, eds. *Skin/Deep: How Race and Complexion Matter in the "Color-Blind" Era.* Chicago: University of Illinois Press, 2004.

Hicks, William. *History of Louisiana Negro Baptists from 1804 to 1914.* Nashville: National Baptist Publishing Board, 1911.

Hunter, Tera W. *To 'Joy My Freedom: Southern Black Women's Lives and Labors after the Civil War.* Cambridge: Harvard University Press, 1997.

Katzman, David M. *Seven Days a Week: Women and Domestic Service in Industrializing America.* Urbana: University of Illinois Press, 1981.

Krenn, Michael. *Black Diplomacy: African Americans and the State Department, 1945-1969.* Armonk: ME Sharpe, 1999.

Leeman, Wayne. "Farmington Teacher's 51-Year Career," *St. Louis Post Dispatch,* May 13, 1954. In Sitzes, "African American History in Farmington."

Lovett, Bobby L. *The African-American History of Nashville, Tennessee, 1780-1930.* Fayetteville: University of Arkansas Press, 1999.

Morrow, E. Frederick. *Black Man in the White House.* New York: Coward-McCann, 1963. "A New Pastor." *Chicago Daily Inter-Ocean,* April 17, 1887.

Nichols, David A. *A Matter of Justice: Eisenhower and the Beginning of the Civil Rights Revolution.* New York: Simon and Schuster, 2007.

Parks, Arnold G. *Lincoln University, 1920-1970.* Charleston, South Carolina: Arcadia Publishing, 2007.

Percy, Anne. *The Early History of Oxford, Mississippi.* Oxford: Percy Enterprises, 2008.

Rawick, George P., Jan Hillegas, and Ken Lawrence. *The American Slave: A Composite Autobiography.* Vol. 10. Westport: Greenwood Press, 1972-79.

Reed, Christopher Robert. *Black Chicago's First Century.* Vol. 1, *1833-1900.* Columbia: University of Missouri Press, 2005.

"Rev. J. B. Wilkins of St. Louis, Yale Graduate, Buried." *St. Louis Argus,* August 12, 1938.

Roberts, Evangeline. "Old Harvard Grad Speaks at Bethesda." *Chicago Defender,* October 29, 1927.

Savage, W. Sherman. *History of Lincoln University.* Jefferson City: Lincoln University Press, 1939.

Sellars, James Benson. *Slavery in Alabama.* Tuscaloosa and London: The University of Alabama Press, 1950.

Siciliano, Rocco. *Walking on Sand.* Salt Lake City: University of Utah Press, 2004.

Sitzes, Faye, ed. "African American History in Farmington." Unpublished collection. Farmington Public Library Genealogy Archives.

"Sixteen-Year-Old Linotypist Sets 40,000 Ems in Day." *St. Louis Argus,* March 30, 1923.

Smith, Jessie Carney. "J. Ernest Wilkins." In *Notable Black American Men.* Detroit: Gale Publications, 1998.

Sollors, Werner, Caldwell Titcomb, and Thomas A. Underwood. *Blacks at Harvard: A Documentary History of African-American Experience at Harvard and Radcliffe.* New York: New York University Press, 1993.

Spear, Allan. *Black Chicago: The Making of a Negro Ghetto – 1890-1920.* Chicago: The University of Chicago Press, 1967.

St. Francois Historical Society. "Interview with Ethelean Cayce, June 27 1984." In Faye Sitzes, ed., "African American History in Farmington."

Strait, Karen K. "139-Year-Old Building Here Once Was Center of Activity for Black Community," *Farmington Forum,* February 14, 1996. In Sitzes, "African American History in Farmington."

Thompson, Patrick. *History of the Negro Baptists in Mississippi.* Jackson, 1898.

Washington, Michael, and Cheryl Nunez. "Education, Racial Uplift and the Rise of the Greek-Letter Tradition." In *African American Fraternities and Sororities: The Legacy and Vision,* ed. Tamara L. Brown, Gregory S. Parks, and Clerenda M. Phillips. Lexington: University Press of Kentucky, 2005.

Who's Who in America, 1952–1853. "J. Ernest Wilkins." Chicago: Marquis, 1952.

Wilkins, J. Ernest. "New Horizons," *Boule Journal*, Vol. 18 #1, October, 1954.

"Wilkins Stymies Reds at Geneva." *Chicago Defender*, June 19, 1954.

Williams, Chad. "Battle Scarred: World War I, African American Officers, and the Fight for Racial Equality." *Africana Heritage* 8 (2008): 8-9.

Williams, Heather Andrea. *Self-Taught: African American Education in Slavery and Freedom*. Chapel Hill: The University of North Carolina Press, 2005.

Williams, Robert Chadwell. *Horace Greeley: Champion of American Freedom*. New York: New York University Press, 2006.

Williamson, Joel. *William Faulkner and Southern History*. New York: Oxford University Press, 1993.

World Methodist Council, United Methodist Church Commission on Archives and History. *Encyclopedia of World Methodism*. Nashville: United Methodist Publishing House, 1960.

Wright, James C. "Porter Family History, Jeffersonville, In." Unpublished manuscript.

Wright, John A., Sr. *The Ville, St. Louis*. Chicago: Arcadia Publishing, 2001.

Internet Sources

AfricanAfricans.com. "A Chronology of African American Military Service." http://www.AfricanAmericans.com/MilitaryChronology3.htm.

The American Experience. "The Murder of Emmett Till." http://www.pbs.org/wgbh/amex/till/index.html.

Billings, Molly. "The Influenza Pandemic of 1918." *Human Virology at Stanford*. http://virus.stanford.edu/uda/.

Cable News Network. "CNN News Report," September 19, 2007. http://www.cnn.com/2007/POLITICS/09/19/jackson.jena6/index.html.

Crocker, Evelyn. "Slave Records of Lafayette County MS." MsGenWeb Project. http://www.theusgenweb.org/ms/lafayette/slave_records.html.

Eisenhower, Dwight D. News conference no. 213, August 20, 1958. http://www.presidency.ucsb.edu/ws/index.php?pid=11178&st=&st1=

Green, Debra Foster. "Just Enough of Everything: The *St. Louis Argus*, an African American Newspaper and Publishing Company in Its First Decade." http://www.hnet.org/~business/bhcweb/publications/BEHonline/2006/greene.pdf 3.

Gudza, Henry P. "James P. Mitchell: Social Conscience of the Cabinet." *Monthly Labor Review*, August 1991. http://www.dol.gov/search/AdvSearch.aspx?agcoll=&taxonomy=&search_term=James+P.+Mitchell&Image1.x=0&Image1.y=0&Image1=Go&offset=0

Israel, Benjamin. "Oldest black newspaper in St. Louis on last legs." *St. Louis Journalism Review*, September 2003. http://goliath.ecnext.com/coms2/summary_0199-3114442_ITM.

Kappa Alpha Psi Fraternity. *A Short Chronicle of Kappa Alpha Psi Fraternity—A Brief History.* http://www.kappaalphapsi1911.com/fraternity/history.asp.

Kappa Alpha Psi Fraternity, Inc. "Laurel Wreath Commission." http://www.kappaalphapsi1911.com/committees/laurel_wreath.asp

Kirkland, Marcus. "The Early History of Farmington." Farmington News Printing Company, 1965. www.rootsweb.ancestry.com.

Lawson, Eric, and Jane Lawson. "Black Yankee: An Interview with Thomas Davis, First World War Veteran." http://worldwarI.com/sfdavis.

Lovett, Bobby L. "Beale Street." *Tennessee Encyclopedia of History and Culture.* Nashville: Tennessee Historical Society, 1998. http://tennesseeencyclopedia.net/imagegallery.php?EntryID=B019

Mayes, Edward. *History of Education in Mississippi.* U.S. Bureau of Education, 1899. http://books.google.com/books?id=MRycAAAAMAAJ&printsec=frontcover&dq=edward+mayes&source=gbs_book

Missouri Digital Heritage Timeline. http://www.sos.mo.gov/archives/resources/africanamerican/timeline/.

Paton, Alan. "The Negro in America Today: South African Novelist Alan Paton Dissects the Racial Situation in the South in the Year of Brown v Board of Education." historymatters.gmu.edu/6337.

Pilgrim Baptist Church. "History." www. pilgrimbaptistchurch.org/history.htm

Public Broadcasting Service. "The Rise and Fall of Jim Crow." http://www.pbs.org/wnet/jimcrow/stories_events_birth.html. Accessed November 20, 2009.

Tipton, Jim. "Lincoln Cemetery." http://www.findagrave.com/php/famous.php?FScemeteryid=106612&page=cem.

Washington, Reginald. "The Freedman's Savings & Trust Company and African American Genealogical Research." *Federal Records and African American History* 29 (Summer 1997). http://www.archives.gov/publications/prologue/1997/summer/freedmans-savings-and-trust.html.

Whitted, J. A. *History of the Negro Baptists of North Carolina.* Raleigh: Broughton Printing, 1908. http://docsouth.unc.edu/church/whitted/menu.html

Vibert, Paul. La nouvelle France catholique. Schleicher Frères, 1908. http://books.google.com/books?id=gXsOAAAAYAAJ.

Additional Sources

Fox News Report, WFNX TV, March 21, 2007.

University of Chicago Registrar. "College Transcript for J. Ernest Wilkins Jr." Chicago, 1937.

Wilkins, J. Ernest. "Toastmaster's Address." Presented during Lincoln University Founders' Day Celebration. Lincoln University, Jefferson City, 1941.

Index